Information Systems Engineering Library

GEMINI Technical Reference

Guidance for KBS development project teams

Frances Scarff

Judith Fynn

CCTA

November 1993

LONDON: HMSO

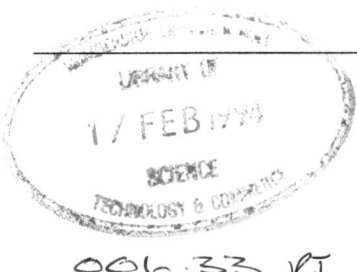

© Crown Copyright 1993

Applications for reproduction should be made to HMSO

First published 1993

ISBN 0 11 330593 1

For further information regarding this publication and other CCTA products please contact:

CCTA Library
Riverwalk House
157-161 Millbank
London SW1P 4RT

071-217-3331

Contents

Foreword

Acknowledgements

1	**Introduction**	**1**

    1.1 Purpose
    1.2 Who should read this publication
    1.3 Structure of this publication
    1.4 How to use this publication
    1.5 GEMINI publications
    1.6 Other publications of interest

2	**Overview of GEMINI concepts**	**7**

    2.1 Special nature of KBS development projects
    2.2 GEMINI guidance
    2.3 Using GEMINI
    2.4 The GEMINI components

3	**GEMINI Components**	**15**

    3.1 Key concepts
    3.2 Project organisation
    3.3 Project management process model
    3.4 Product-oriented framework
    3.5 Summary

4	**Product Breakdown Structure**	**27**

    4.1 Introduction
    4.2 An exemplar Product Breakdown Structure
    4.3 Diagramming conventions
    4.4 Top-level product breakdown
    4.5 Management Products Breakdown
    4.6 Technical Products Breakdown
    4.7 Quality Products Breakdown
    4.8 Application Products Breakdown
    4.9 Summary

5		**Product descriptions**	**47**

- 5.1 Introduction
- 5.2 Product description format
- 5.3 Described products
- 5.4 Activity description
- 5.5 Application Requirements Model
- 5.6 Business Domain Model
- 5.7 Circuit Initiation Document (CID)
- 5.8 Expertise Model
- 5.9 Feasibility Report
- 5.10 Functional Design Model
- 5.11 Logical Analysis Model
- 5.12 Management Risk Assessment
- 5.13 Modality Model
- 5.14 Physical Design Model
- 5.15 Physical Environment Specification
- 5.16 Physical System Specification
- 5.17 Plan
- 5.18 Product Breakdown Structure (PBS)
- 5.19 Product description
- 5.20 Product Flow Diagram
- 5.21 Progress Report
- 5.22 Project Initiation Document (PID)
- 5.23 Rejected Technical Environment Options
- 5.24 Selected Application Model
- 5.25 Technical Environment Description
- 5.26 Technical Environment Options
- 5.27 Work structure

6		**Work structures**	**129**

- 6.1 Introduction
- 6.2 High-level Product Flow Diagram
- 6.3 Work structure
- 6.4 Control points
- 6.5 Activity description format
- 6.6 Summary

| 7 | Activity descriptions | 141 |

    7.1 Introduction
    7.2 Feasibility Study (FS) activity description
    7.3 Requirements Analysis (RA) activity description
    7.4 System Modelling (SM) activity description
    7.5 Logical Analysis (LA) activity description
    7.6 Logical Design (LD) activity description
    7.7 Technical Environment Definition (TE) activity description
    7.8 Physical Design (PD) activity description

| 8 | Techniques | 183 |

    8.1 Introduction
    8.2 Knowledge acquisition techniques
    8.3 Knowledge representation techniques
    8.4 KBS validation techniques
    8.5 Generally applicable techniques
    8.6 Technique selection
    8.7 Summary

Annexes

| A | Risk management issues | 223 |

    A.1 Categories of risk
    A.2 Project initiation
    A.3 Main development phase
    A.4 Project closure and beyond
    A.5 Demand-supply relationship

| B | Techniques list | 235 |

Bibliography   243

Glossary   249

Index   261

GEMINI Technical Reference

Foreword

The **Information Systems Engineering Library** provides guidance on managing and carrying out Information Systems Engineering activities. In the IS life cycle, Information Systems Engineering takes place once the IS strategy has been defined. It is concerned with the development and ongoing improvement of information systems up to the operational stage, when systems become the responsibility of infrastructure management.

The Information Systems Engineering Library builds on guidance in the CCTA IS Guides, particularly set A: *Management and Planning Set* and set B: *Systems Development Set* and complements other CCTA products, in particular the project management method, PRINCE, and the systems analysis and design method, SSADM.

Volumes in the Information Systems Engineering Library are of interest to varying levels of staff from IS directors to IS providers, helping them to improve the quality and productivity of their IS development work. Some volumes in this library should also be of interest to business managers, IS users and those involved in market testing, whose business operations depend on having effective IS support by means of Information Systems Engineering activities.

The Information Systems Engineering Library also complements other related CCTA publications, particularly the IT Infrastructure Library for operational issues and the IS Planning Subject Guides for strategic issues.

CCTA welcomes customer views on Information Systems Engineering Library publications. Please send your comments to:

Customer Services
Information Systems Engineering Group
Gildengate House
Upper Green Lane
NORWICH
NR3 1DW

Acknowledgements

The GEMINI guidance has been developed using a wide range of expertise from the following:

> Chris Harris-Jones and David Hannaford from BIS Information Systems Ltd.
>
> Mark Thomas and Ebbi Adhami from Ernst & Young Management Consultants.
>
> Paul Shufflebottom from LBMS plc.
>
> Jim Kennedy and Marc Foote from Logica (Cambridge Ltd).
>
> Steve Cogbill from Logica Research and Defence.
>
> Richard Susskind from Masons.
>
> Gary Borne from SD-Scicon.
>
> Frank Hickman, Jonathan Killin and Lise Land from Touche Ross Management Consultants.

Contributions have been made by reviewers from a wide range of Government Depts including:

> Department of Health
>
> Department of Trade and Industry
>
> HM Customs and Excise
>
> Inland Revenue
>
> ITSA
>
> MOD AQUILA

Contributions have been made by reviewers from academic institutions including:

> AIAI
>
> Liverpool University (Dept. of Computer Science)

Acknowledgements

Contributions have been made by reviewers from a wide range of commercial organisations including:

British Aerospace

British Telecom (Martlesham Heath)

Inference (Europe)

Norwich Union

Siemens Nixdorf Information Systems

GEMINI Technical Reference

1 Introduction

1.1 Purpose

This publication provides technical information to enable KBS developers to contribute to or work within the well-defined planning framework that GEMINI provides. The guidance needs to be tailored for each individual KBS project.

Development projects for *knowledge based systems* (KBS) require the use of novel analysis and design techniques. The development process frequently involves an iterative approach to knowledge acquisition, requirements analysis and design. KBS projects are therefore not fully amenable to conventional methods for development and project management.

The purpose of the GEMINI volumes of the Information Systems Engineering Library is to help organisations adapt their project practices for KBS development. Within GEMINI, the analysis and design elements are based on good practice for KBS development. The project management approach is based on the government preferred project management method Projects IN Controlled Environments (PRINCE).

1.2 Who should read this publication

This publication is primarily intended for *KBS development practitioners* involved in projects being managed according to GEMINI guidance.

This publication is of interest to:

- KBS development teams
- KBS project managers
- any member of a KBS development project who needs to understand the technical aspects of GEMINI.

GEMINI Technical Reference

1.3	**Structure of this publication**	Chapter 2 provides an overview of GEMINI concepts and structure.

Chapter 3 describes the components of GEMINI. These components are expanded in detail in subsequent chapters.

Chapters 4 and 5 document a set of products to be produced by a project run in accordance with the GEMINI guidance.

Chapters 6 and 7 concentrate on the activities needed to develop the products required by a KBS development project.

Chapter 8 describes some of the techniques that can be used during the product development process.

1.4	**How to use this publication**	GEMINI provides a generic approach to undertaking KBS development projects. It is designed to be flexible rather than prescriptive and is intended to be adapted to the particular needs of the organisations which use it and of the projects to which it is applied.

GEMINI includes PRINCE concepts tailored for KBS development projects, and some additional concepts. It is assumed that the reader has knowledge of PRINCE. A full explanation of the method is available in the PRINCE manuals.

Organisations which use a project management method other than PRINCE will need to determine how their approach needs to be modified to allow it to be used in conjunction with GEMINI.

The GEMINI Technical Reference volume can be read selectively to provide an understanding of the technicalities of the GEMINI components. This volume is the central reference for the technical aspects of the concepts embodied in GEMINI.

Chapter 1
Introduction

The volume is to be used in conjunction with either of the companion volumes, as described in section 1.5, to support two types of activity:

- planning/monitoring
- development.

Planning/monitoring
This volume can be used to help with the initial project planning for a KBS project when decisions need to be made on which techniques to use and how the project will proceed.

These decisions, together with organisational considerations, can help with the adaptation of GEMINI to meet the project's needs.

GEMINI advocates controlled management of risk. The major emphasis is on frequent cycles of review, risk assessment and planning.

Development
The publication gives guidance to practitioners on what should be produced and the dependencies between products.

The publication also suggests how products can be developed and the appropriate techniques to use.

1.5 GEMINI publications

This publication is one of three volumes which together form the foundation volumes of the GEMINI guidance within the CCTA Information System Engineering (ISE) Library. The others are:

- *GEMINI: Controlling KBS Development Projects - Guidance for business-side project controllers*
- *GEMINI: Managing KBS Development Projects - Guidance for IS-provider project managers.*

GEMINI Technical Reference

Each of these volumes is intended to be self contained; therefore, some information is duplicated across the volumes. Each volume holds an appropriate level of detail for its purpose, and each volume contains an index which can help to:

- direct the reader to specific text
- identify duplicated coverage of information on a particular topic.

Although GEMINI has been produced as guidance for KBS developments, many of the concepts can be applied to any project which is innovative, risk prone and requires iterative development. However, when GEMINI is used for non-KBS projects, it must be tailored to fit those projects. The KBS-specific products, development activities and techniques defined in GEMINI will need to be redefined appropriately for the type of project.

The GEMINI publications contain general concepts which are explained more fully in other CCTA publications. Information on these concepts is included in the GEMINI publications to set the context and reduce the need to reference other documents, especially the PRINCE manuals. Some of the relevant publications are described in section 1.6.

GEMINI: Controlling KBS Development Projects

GEMINI: Controlling KBS Development Projects defines the roles required for KBS projects in addition to the standard PRINCE roles. It gives an understanding of the key issues involved in controlling the development of KBS and the steps needed to ensure these are addressed. *GEMINI: Controlling KBS Development Projects* is addressed primarily at the business user organisation.

Chapter 1
Introduction

GEMINI: Managing KBS Development Projects	*GEMINI: Managing KBS Development Projects* gives Project Managers an understanding of the key issues involved in developing KBS and helps them ensure that KBS projects are managed and undertaken correctly. *GEMINI: Managing KBS Development Projects* is addressed primarily at the IS-provider organisation.

1.6 Other publications of interest

Other CCTA publications may be of interest to those using GEMINI guidance. These include the Appraisal and Evaluation Library which includes a volume specific to KBS software tools. Other related publications are concerned with the PRINCE project management method, quality management, CCTA Risk Analysis and Management Method (CRAMM) and the IT Infrastructure Library (ITIL).

PRINCE Manuals

PRINCE is the recommended project management method for use in government. It comprises an integrated set of procedures based on a number of key principles. There is a set of five manuals which document the PRINCE approach to project management.

Some PRINCE concepts have been detailed in GEMINI to limit the requirement to reference the PRINCE manuals. For adoption of a non-PRINCE like project management method, further PRINCE information may be needed to allow a complete understanding of the project management principles embodied in GEMINI.

Appraisal and Evaluation Library

The Appraisal and Evaluation Library helps organisations to identify the products, particularly software, which best meet their requirements. It consists of a general procedures volume, which describes an appraisal and evaluation 'method', followed by a number of technology specific volumes. There is a volume on KBS, which provides a hierarchy of criteria that may be used as the basis for the evaluation of KBS tools.

CRAMM   CRAMM provides a structured and consistent basis to
                            identify and justify all the protective measures
                            necessary to ensure the security of both current and
                            future IT systems used for processing data.

                            CRAMM can be used within a KBS development
                            project to establish requirements and constraints
                            associated with security.

IT Infrastructure   The IT Infrastructure Library (ITIL) is a set of guidance
Library   books which give a comprehensive structured approach
                            to providing IT services and the accommodation and
                            environmental facilities needed to support IT. The
                            publications bring together best IT practices within the
                            public and private sector. These documents cover a
                            variety of subjects, some of which are of direct
                            relevance to GEMINI, including:

                            • Capacity Management

                            • Change Management

                            • Configuration Management

                            • Testing an IT Service for Operational Use.

Quality Management   The Quality Management Library provides guidance on
Library   implementing and supporting quality management
                            systems (QMS) within IS organisations.

2 Overview of GEMINI concepts

2.1 Special nature of KBS development projects

Knowledge based system (KBS) development projects involve the use of novel analysis and design techniques and an iterative development approach. Therefore KBS projects are not fully amenable to conventional methods for software development and project management.

Conventional methods do not meet the needs of KBS development projects for three main reasons:

- special techniques are required for knowledge acquisition and representation
- the activities of feasibility study, analysis and design may overlap
- KBS development projects are generally innovative and thus, particularly susceptible to risk.

In any information systems development, there is a progression from defining what the IS customer - the *demand side* - needs, to how the systems are actually provided by the *supply side*.

Special techniques

KBS are concerned with capturing and using knowledge and expertise which may previously only have been available from human sources. The developed system may replace interaction with a human expert. A requirement to deliver expertise is met by analysis of the knowledge and translation of the results of the analysis into the implemented system. Specialised techniques are required, especially in the area of acquisition of knowledge and its subsequent representation.

The comparative novelty of some of the techniques means that the development team requires specialised skills not widely available.

The issues above highlight the importance of effective communication between the demand side and the supply side, especially when there is more than one supplier participating within a single project. This increases the complexity of project control.

Overlapping activities

The full definition of the functionality of a KBS can only be achieved after discussion with experts in the domain of the proposed application and with potential users of the implemented system. The feasibility and scope of the system may have to be revised at a relatively late stage in the project.

It is not usually possible to separate the activities of analysis, design and implementation into a clean linear sequence, as required by a waterfall lifecycle. Some revision of the design and even the analysis products may occur late in the project as the scope and limitations of expert knowledge emerge.

Each product of the development project depends on the availability of information required as input to the appropriate development activity, often from another product. This type of dependency between products needs to be identified. The ordering and conduct of activities should be determined by the characteristics, dependencies and needs of individual projects.

In this situation, it is extremely important for the demand side to keep tight control over resource usage and to monitor progress.

Project risk

The successful use of KBS can result in great benefits in business areas previously intractable to IT. An unacceptably high proportion of KBS projects still fail to deliver operational systems which meet business requirements, to time and within budget.

KBS require the use of innovative development techniques whose use makes the project risk-prone There may be difficulties in assessing technical feasibility and estimating resource requirements, which increases the probability of missed delivery and budget targets.

Chapter 2
Overview of GEMINI concepts

KBS can support executive functions fundamental to the business aims. If the KBS were to give imperfect information or fail to perform the desired function adequately, this could prove detrimental to the whole business.

Many conventional project management methods incorporate elements of risk control, though these elements are not often openly described. KBS developments require risk analysis and re-planning to be made explicit in the project control process.

2.2 GEMINI guidance

GEMINI guidance focuses on the organisational and planning framework to control KBS developments with the aim of addressing the areas where conventional methods fail to tackle the issues highlighted in section 2.1.

GEMINI provides a flexible approach for management and control which incorporates continuous risk management and allows the development team to employ the techniques and methods appropriate to the project. The scope of GEMINI encompasses Feasibility Study through design, covering the issues specific to KBS. The guidance must be tailored to fit existing standards for the organisation and to meet the needs of individual projects.

Key design features of GEMINI include:

- usability
- flexibility
- rigour
- quality.

Usability	The test of any guidance is the extent to which it is found useful in practice. Therefore, the design aim is to ensure that GEMINI guidance:

- *is understandable* for those with a background in conventional IT
- can be widely *taught* and easily *learned*
- is *applicable* in a wide range of different situations: for example, it is able to address different business problems or different technical constraints
- is *tailorable* so that the activities carried out are relevant to the project in question. |
| Flexibility | GEMINI guidance provides a flexible approach for management and control which incorporates continuous risk management. It also allows the development team to employ the techniques and methods most appropriate to the project. |
| Rigour | GEMINI is designed to allow:

- project objectives to be set, linking demonstrably to business objectives
- products which support project objectives to be identified during planning
- product development to be monitored and documented, which helps to ensure that products are developed efficiently and economically
- risks to project objectives to be rigorously assessed and effectively controlled. |
| Quality | GEMINI embodies good practice in KBS development. Management techniques used for conventional developments are adopted, where appropriate, and if necessary enhanced. |

Chapter 2
Overview of GEMINI concepts

GEMINI emphasises the management of quality. Quality is achieved by identifying:

- what needs to be produced
- how production will be undertaken
- activities to be scheduled, with particular reference to quality review.

Everyone involved in the project should be aware of these requirements and their part in the quality assurance process.

2.3 Using GEMINI

Using GEMINI involves substantial preparatory work in the early stages of a project. This work sets the baseline and the framework for the project, which will then be driven by:

- an understanding and assessment of objectives and constraints
- the assessment and management of risk
- the assessment and management of quality.

Planning, monitoring and control of a project have their own resource requirements but are necessary for the developed system to meet its business objectives.

2.4 The GEMINI components

GEMINI guidance consists of the following key components:

- a project organisation structure
- a project management process model with risk management fully integrated
- a product-oriented framework to identify the products to be developed and the activities to develop them.

2.4.1 Project organisation structure

A GEMINI-based project has a clearly defined project management environment. A project organisation structure is detailed in Chapter 3.

2.4.2 Project management process model

Project management is concerned with the deployment and control of all resources assigned to the project to ensure efficient and economical delivery of effective systems.

Rigorous risk management has been incorporated into GEMINI because KBS developments are more threatened by risks than many conventional IT projects.

After each risk assessment, development work is planned, carried out and reviewed.

The process model takes account of the iterative nature of KBS development. This mode of development and the process model are described in Chapter 3.

2.4.3 Product-oriented framework

The framework provided by GEMINI defines the products needed to support the development of KBS. This framework includes products for use in:

- management and control of the project (Management Products)
- translating the initial business requirements through analysis and design into an implemented system (Technical Products)
- quality control (Quality Products).

The division of products into these three categories is reflected in the GEMINI example Product Breakdown Structure (PBS). This PBS is documented in Chapter 4.

The Technical Products include the analysis and design products which represent knowledge during the *knowledge transformation process*.

Knowledge transformation

The knowledge to be encapsulated into a KBS is held, prior to analysis, in human minds or documentation of rules and procedures. The final KBS holds knowledge in a form appropriate to the hardware and software environment in which it is implemented. The transformation from the former to the latter is the process of analysis and design. This process can be seen as a series of translations from the business requirement through various analyses of the requirements and designs of the system to the solution in the form of an operational system. The transformation process is documented in the Technical Products.

The main Technical Products are outlined in Chapter 4. A description of the full range of GEMINI products is given in Chapter 5.

Work structure

The products need to be incorporated into a structure which allows activities for development to be defined and shows the inter-relationships between products and activities. These inter-relationships are documented in a work structure. The work structure focuses on the technical activities carried out in a GEMINI-based project, though the management and quality activities are also reflected.

The work structures and project activities are described in Chapters 6 and 7. These chapters describe possible activities to develop the products for a typical GEMINI-based project.

2.4.4 Exemplar descriptions

All the descriptions referenced above are exemplars which should be tailored to determine the conduct of, and the products for, each individual project.

3 GEMINI Components

3.1 Key concepts

GEMINI provides a basis for the development of knowledge based systems. It provides guidance on *what* should be produced rather than *how* it should be produced. This chapter describes the GEMINI components and explains how they are used for a knowledge based system development project.

Project organisation

Within GEMINI, *project organisation* is the composition of a team in terms of the skills and experience required to undertake all the necessary functions of control, management and development within a project. The project functions are assigned to a number of designated *roles*. These roles are assigned to individuals according to the needs of the project and the mix of skills available.

Each individual undertaking a role must:

- have appropriate skills and knowledge for the allocated role

- understand their responsibilities and those of the other project members, which includes understanding the requirements for interaction with other roles

- understand the project organisation structure and reporting lines.

An exemplar project organisation structure is detailed in section 3.2.

Project management process model

A GEMINI-based project is undertaken as an initial review followed by a sequence of risk assessment, planning, development and review. This concept is portrayed in the spiral model for the project management process. This model emphasises the management of risk, and is explained in section 3.3.

Using a spiral model ensures that consideration of project objectives and risks to them are regularly examined. Further action is planned to keep the project on track and to monitor progress.

Product-oriented framework A variety of information covering management, technical and quality issues must be collated for a project to run successfully. All this information needs to be captured in a form suitable for its proposed use. GEMINI focuses on the products required to build the required KBS. These products are developed by the project activities. For more details, see section 3.4.

3.2 Project organisation

A GEMINI-based project has a clearly defined project management environment. This section describes the recommended organisation structure, and explains the roles particularly significant for members of the development team or additional to standard PRINCE.

Figure 3.1 illustrates the GEMINI recommended organisation structure and shows the split of functions between the demand and supply sides.

A potential need has been established by the demand side. The supply side meets this need, by undertaking development of the full KBS, or some aspect of the development.

The demand side runs the project and controls the demand/supply interface. The supply side may also run the work as part of a separate project within their own organisation.

Section 3.2 concentrates on the overall project. Any discussion of the project organisation in the rest of this volume refers to that controlled by the demand side, which excludes the shaded area of the diagram.

Chapter 3
GEMINI Components

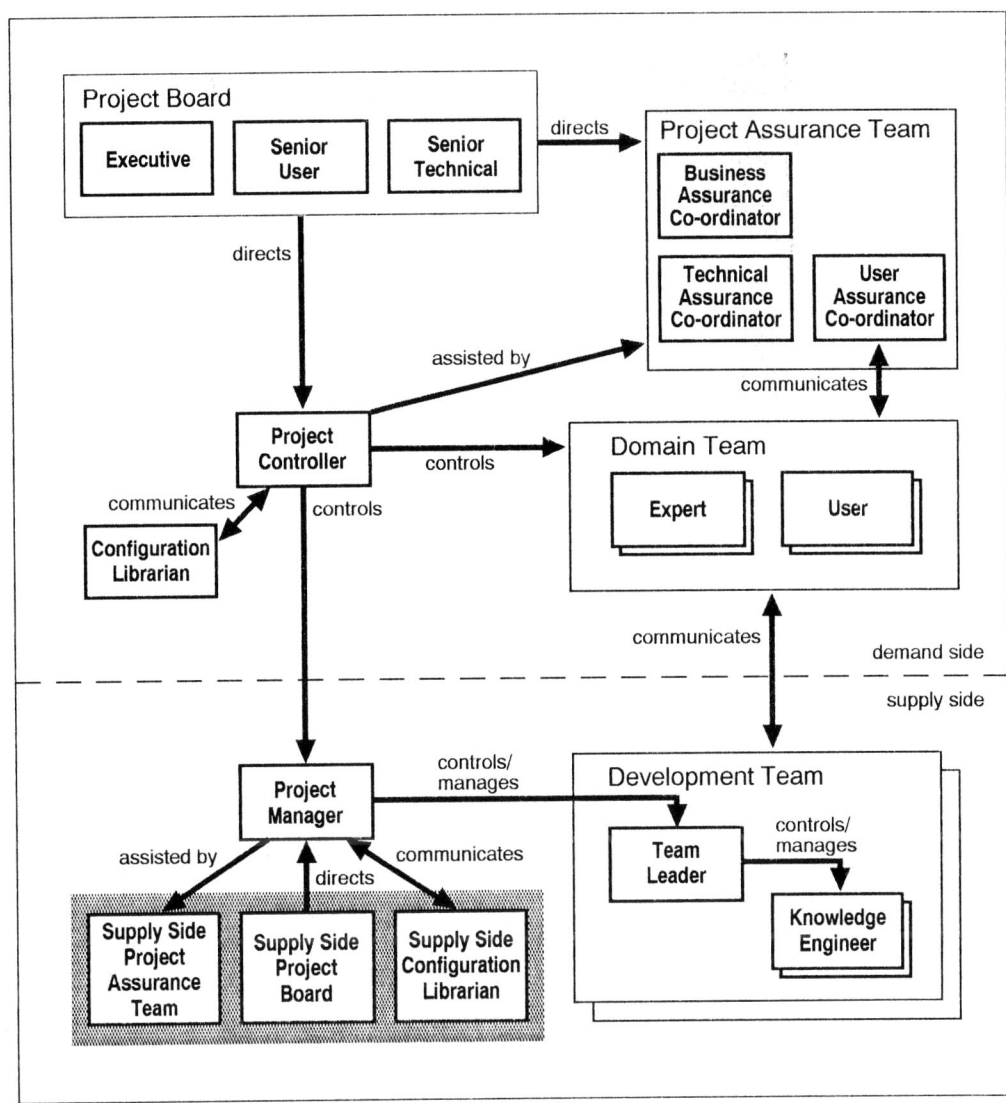

Figure 3.1: Organisation Structure for a GEMINI project

3.2.1 Project Board

The *Project Board* is the group of senior managers on the demand side, who have an interest in, and overall control of, the KBS project. The Project Board must provide overall guidance and direction to the project. The members of the Project Board must have sufficient authority to commit resources from their appropriate areas.

3.2.2 Project Controller

The *Project Controller* is the demand side project manager responsible for the success of the project in terms of quality of the delivered system, within the project's budget and timescale.

The Project Controller is responsible for controlling the demand/supply interface and monitoring the delivery of those project products which the supply side is responsible for developing.

3.2.3 Domain Team

The *Domain Team* is the group of people from the business who have or use the knowledge which the KBS is to contain. The Domain Team provides information for the analysis and design activities carried out by the Development Team. Some of the Domain Team gain benefit from the project in their day-to-day activities once the application has been analysed and built.

There are two groups of Domain Team candidates of particular interest:

- Users
- Experts.

User

The *User* is the group of users, or their representative, who makes direct use of the final implemented system.

Expert

The *Expert* is a group of experts, or their representative, who currently perform the function which the system will eventually provide. The Expert will be made available to be interviewed for knowledge analysis purposes.

The Expert provides the materials, including specialist knowledge, documentation and case studies, that are required by the Knowledge Engineers. In some cases the Expert may be involved in system testing.

Experts may also be prospective users of the final implemented system. If so, the expert, acting as user, is likely to have different needs to those of other users.

3.2.4 Project Manager

The *Project Manager* has responsibility for the overall management of the supply side activities with additional responsibility for providing information to the demand side.

3.2.5 Development Team

A Project Manager is supported by at least one *Development Team* which is responsible for delivering the products of the project. These roles have the same overall function as a development team on a non-KBS project. Different skills are required to undertake these functions which relate directly to the techniques and technology being employed.

Team Leader

The *Team Leader* has to manage the development of particular products using specified resources. The Team Leader requires the skills to be able to lead and co-ordinate a team of Knowledge Engineers. Typically, the Team Leader is a working member of the Development Team.

The Team Leader must be proficient in the use of KBS development techniques. A thorough knowledge of the relevant aspects of GEMINI concerning the development of the specific product(s) is essential.

Knowledge Engineer

Knowledge Engineers are the main body of development personnel in a KBS project. They carry out the analysis, design and programming activities of a KBS development.

GEMINI Technical Reference

GEMINI guidance does not cover coding and implementation of the system. Programming expertise is an essential skill where prototyping is being used to support the analysis and design process.

3.2.6 Further information

A more complete description of the project organisation can be found in the companion volume *GEMINI: Controlling KBS Development Projects*.

3.3 Project management process model

The *project management process model*, (the spiral model), shows how management and control can be imposed on a KBS project, while allowing several development models to be produced in parallel.

3.3.1 Project management process

Each major activity within a project starts with a review when the overall scope of the major activity is defined.

The initial review is followed by a sequence of risk assessment, planning, development and review. This concept is shown in Figure 3.2, with the main topics for consideration at each point in the sequence.

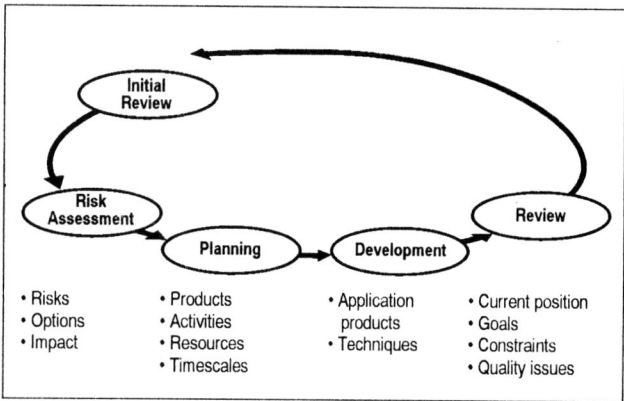

Figure 3.2: The project management processes

The sequence is repeated until all the development activities are complete.

3.3.2 Spiral model

A project is carried out through repetition of the sequence of project management processes. Each iteration of the sequence should yield progress in:

- degree of understanding of outstanding risk
- accuracy of future plans and estimates
- development of the implementable KBS
- quality, that is, assuring the fitness for purpose of products.

The iteration of the project management process sequence can be represented graphically as a spiral. A passage through all four sectors comprises a circuit of the spiral.

This spiral is illustrated in Figure 3.3.

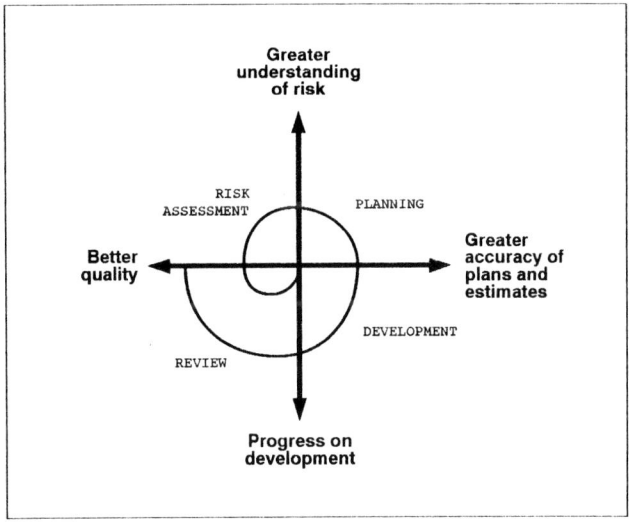

Figure 3.3: Project management process model

The division of the spiral into four sectors does not imply an equal distribution of time or other resources through the sectors.

GEMINI Technical Reference

Initial review

Objectives and constraints are identified during the *initial review* to set the scope for the rest of the spiral. These details must be adequately documented in a Project Initiation Document (PID) before the work covered by the spiral can start.

The details in the PID are used as the baseline for the whole project.

Risk assessment sector

All major risks are identified or reassessed during the *risk assessment sector*.

All issues which could jeopardise the success of the project need to be considered. An assessment has to be made of impact on the outcome of the project. Resolution options need to be formulated, ramifications identified and their practicality assessed.

Planning sector

During the *planning sector*, the plans are created or adjusted in accordance with changes suggested by the risk assessment and to reflect progress made. This planning may require the update of overall plans, as well as the production of detailed technical, resource and quality plans for the activities to be undertaken within the next development sector. Plans should be formulated or adjusted to take account of chosen risk resolution options.

Development sector

The analysis, design and construction activities take place during the *development sector*. This sector will have a longer elapsed time than the other sectors and consume more resources. Its outputs are the Technical Products and progress reports which pass into the review exercise.

Review sector

During the *review sector*, the quality and impact of products produced to date are examined and the next set of project objectives and constraints identified.

The outputs from the review represent major issues for the other sectors to address.

3.3.3 Further information — Using the principles embodied within the spiral model is part of the project management activities. More detail concerning use of the spiral model is given in Chapter 4 of each of the companion volumes.

3.4 Product-oriented framework

The product-oriented framework requires that the products to be developed and their logical dependencies are identified. The framework details the mechanisms used to inform management of project progress.

A project requires the development of products to support management and control functions in addition to the Technical Products. Details of the required products are given in Chapters 4 and 5.

The Technical Products are primarily concerned with transforming knowledge from requirement to solution.

3.4.1 Knowledge transformation

An approach to KBS development which relied upon transforming application specific knowledge directly into implementation specific representations would be very tedious indeed, since each transformation would be unique to that application. In addition, the implementation specific representation would bias the analysis and interpretation of the knowledge. The application specific knowledge would be made to fit the implementation specific representation.

GEMINI guidance is intended to be used for projects in a wide range of application areas, with each implemented using the most appropriate technology.

Products of the early parts of a project need to be represented in a way which is largely dependent on the characteristics of the type of application (application specific). Products in the latter parts of a project need to be represented in a way conducive to the technology to be used for implementation (implementation specific).

Thus, in GEMINI, inferences are first identified as being representative of a specific type of knowledge and then abstracted to a form and structure which is quite independent of their origin. Once this analysis is complete, the choice of representation for the implementation environment, for example rules and frames, can be made based on the requirements of the application rather than on the way in which the application requirements are expressed.

GEMINI development models represent different stages in the translation process. The products of the early part of the project may be highly application specific in the way they are represented. Products during the latter stages tend to be dependent on the technology used to implement the final system.

3.4.2 Development models

The eight development models listed below are the high-level analysis and design products to be delivered during a GEMINI-based KBS development project:

- Business Domain Model
- Selected Application Model
- Application Requirements Model
- Expertise Model
- Modality Model
- Logical Analysis Model
- Functional Design Model
- Physical Design Model.

These eight development models are defined in Chapters 4 and 5.

It is necessary to produce high-level versions of some of these development models to assess the feasibility of the project. In particular, the Business Domain Model and the Application Requirements Model are likely to be outlined during a Feasibility Study. This outlining is necessary to scope the project requirements. Feasibility is assessed in terms of business, organisation and technical viability. The findings of the Feasibility Study are documented in a Feasibility Report.

3.4.3 GEMINI knowledge definition

The requirements to be analysed for a KBS must cover all the specialised and non-specialised knowledge, which is required for the application to perform the intended purpose. The knowledge needs to have identified boundaries. This bounded knowledge is called the *domain* of the KBS.

It is necessary to determine the way in which the system will be used, as the KBS user may be a non-expert or someone who uses it infrequently. The KBS, in this instance, must be easy to use and guide the user through its functions. In certain situations, the user may need the KBS to explain the way a particular conclusion has been reached. These aspects affect the overall usability of the KBS.

3.5 Summary

To support the successful undertaking of a KBS development project, GEMINI details the project organisation and advocates deployment of the spiral model to address project management.

For analysis and design, GEMINI identifies a set of development models that effect the transformation from an application specific representation into an implementation specific representation.

The knowledge which is to be encoded into the KBS must have identifiable boundaries so that its completeness can be assessed. Consideration must also be given to the requirements of the users of the final implemented system.

GEMINI Technical Reference

4 Product Breakdown Structure

4.1 Introduction

This chapter provides information on the products to be produced as part of a GEMINI-based project. The chapter is particularly concerned with the way in which these products fit together and provide full documentation of the project.

Product Breakdown Structure (PBS)

A variety of information covering management, technical and quality issues must be collated for a project to run successfully. The *Product Breakdown Structure* (PBS) is a hierarchy of the products to be produced to hold all the required information for a project.

Each product in the PBS hierarchy should be included for a clearly understood purpose. The PBS must be approved by the Project Board so that the development of each product can be planned. The PBS is supported by a set of product descriptions which cover all the products identified in the PBS.

The spiral model, deployed within the GEMINI framework, highlights the need for risk assessment and review of the project and the development of products. The PBS includes products to document these activities formally.

The exemplar PBS within this chapter represents the products likely to be necessary for a typical KBS development project. This PBS can be used as a base for actual projects but requires tailoring to each project's needs.

Project scope

The exemplar PBS is based on the assumption that the described project covers all activities from initial inception through to final system implementation. This range of activities may be achieved as three separate projects:

- Feasibility Study
- Full Study (requirements analysis and logical design)
- system development and implementation.

GEMINI does not cover implementation or maintenance products directly. The GEMINI products provide a basis for implementation and maintenance activities which are similar to those of conventional IT. These products are included on the PBS for completeness but are not described in detail within GEMINI.

4.2 An exemplar Product Breakdown Structure

This chapter describes the products of a typical KBS development project. Many products consist of several simpler products, which are composed of still simpler products. Structure diagrams illustrate this decomposition beginning at the very highest level, Project Products. This top-level represents the sum total of all products required in a project to hold all the required information.

The PBS needs to be tailored to specific installation standards, with the proviso that the information content needs to be consistent with GEMINI guidance.

The products are split into three areas of information:

- management
- quality
- technical.

Chapter 4
Product Breakdown Structure

All the GEMINI development models are contained within the Application Products Breakdown, which is a subset of Technical Products. The detailed representation of these models, which depends on the specific techniques used for their development, is not covered by GEMINI. However the high-level descriptions in this guidance facilitate the use of GEMINI in conjunction with other methods appropriate to the particular project.

Product descriptions (see Chapter 5) explain the purpose and content of the products which are particularly important in GEMINI or differ from standard IT project products.

4.3 Diagramming conventions

The following conventions have been used within the Product Breakdown Structure documented in this chapter.

notation	interpretation
Name (box)	name of product.
(stacked boxes)	shows that several versions of this product exist over time. Generally, these indicate some sort of historical record of events. The most recent is usually the most relevant to the current activities of the project.
———	shows the composition of the higher-level product by showing which component products make up the higher product.
fn.n (circle)	identifies the figure where further information concerning this object can be found, as *fn.n*. The first number identifies the chapter and the second number identifies the figure within the chapter. This signposting works both up and down the hierarchy of figures.

The first three conventions reflect the PRINCE approach to drawing any PBS. The fourth convention, signposting between figures, is specifically for use in this publication. Ideally, a PBS would be drawn as a single figure and thus obviate the need for such signposting.

4.4　Top-level product breakdown

The top-level of the PBS has the three elements which reflect the breakdown of the products within a management planning and control method, such as PRINCE. See Figure 4.1.

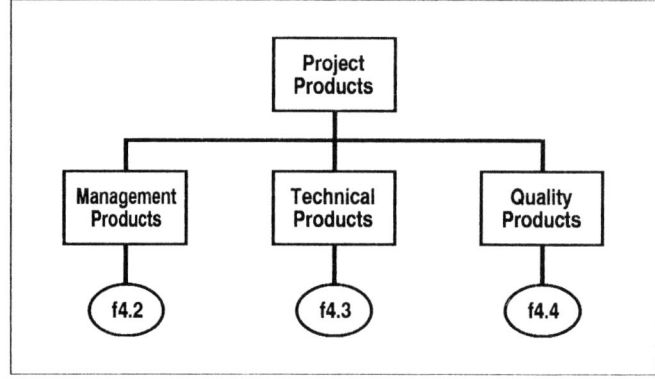

Figure 4.1: Project Products Breakdown Structure

The three categories of product, while different, are complementary and are all needed to ensure that a high-quality solution is provided in a managed and controlled manner.

Management Products are used in the management of the project and focus on planning and control aspects. See section 4.5 for further details.

Technical Products are the results of the project development activities. See section 4.6 for further details.

Quality Products show that quality has been built into the process of developing the system. In particular, product descriptions contain quality criteria which must be met by the developed products if they are to serve their designated purpose. See section 4.7 for further details.

Chapter 4
Product Breakdown Structure

4.5 Management Products Breakdown

Management Products Breakdown consists of those products necessary for the planning and control of the project. See Figure 4.2.

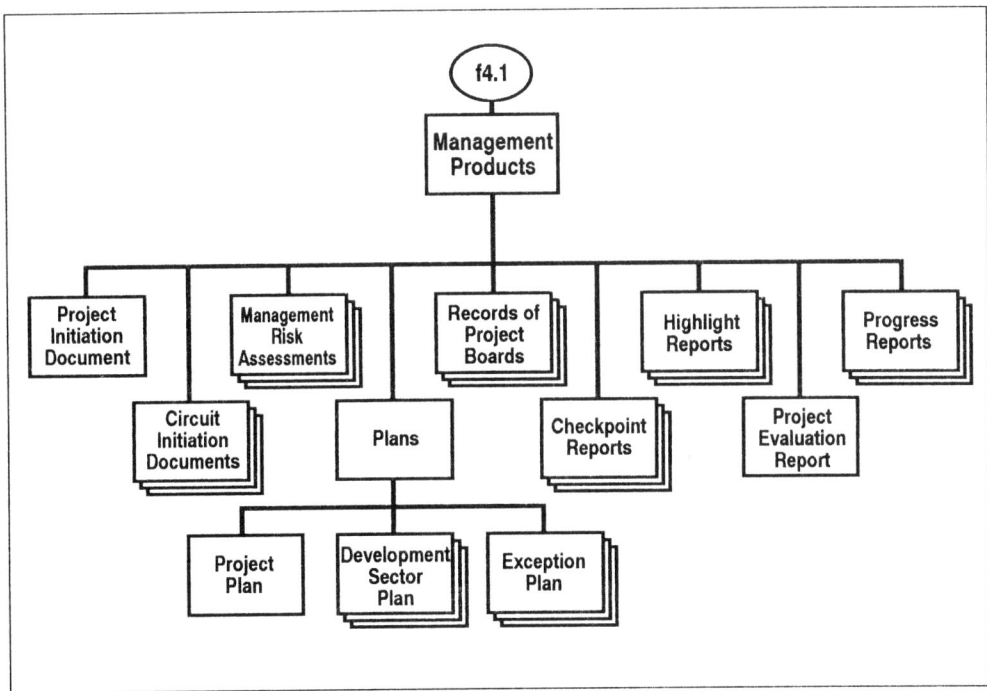

Figure 4.2: Management Products Breakdown Structure

Project Initiation Document

Some information must be drawn together before a project can formally start. Management must agree the project scope and objectives and show how these fit within the business objectives. This information is documented in the *Project Initiation Document* (PID). This product must be available for reference throughout the project.

An important element of a PID is the *terms of reference* within which the project activities must be undertaken.

Circuit Initiation Documents	Objectives and boundaries of the activities for each circuit of the project management process model (spiral model) need to be documented. The *Circuit Initiation Document* (CID) for the following circuit of the spiral model is developed at the end of each review process. Management approval of this product is required before the next circuit of the spiral can commence.

These details must be within the *project boundary* as set out in the PID and consistent with it. The latest CID forms the current project baseline and scopes the next circuit of the spiral. In this context, the CID is used during the next review phase to assess the progress which has been made in the current spiral circuit. |
| Management Risk Assessment | There are risks to the project's business, technical or organisational viability. Each potential risk must be identified and assessed in terms of probability and likely impact. Possible options for reducing risk must be identified and evaluated. Management must make an assessment of the feasibility of addressing these risks within the project's terms of reference. The relevant information is documented in the *Management Risk Assessment*. |
| Plans | *Plans* consist of the documents which are produced during the project planning process and updated as a result of subsequent control processes.

Plans are not single documents, see Chapter 5: Product descriptions. In particular, a plan includes technical, resource and quality aspects.

Initially, a plan documents estimated resource usage. The plan forms a baseline established during planning and agreed by management. The plan is updated with actual details as the project progresses. These changes to a plan highlight allowed tolerance levels that have been, or are about to be, exceeded. |

The *Project Plan* shows how the GEMINI approach and appropriate techniques are to be used to conduct the project. It will, therefore, show the products to be developed and the associated activities specific to the project concerned, together with overall estimates. The Project Plan is updated, during each review sector of the project spiral, as the project progresses. The amended Project Plan shows how resources were expended and a revised view of the expected resource requirements for the rest of the project.

A *Development Sector Plan*, produced during a planning sector, schedules the detailed resources required to develop the products covered by the current circuit of the spiral and carry out associated review activities.

An *Exception Plan* documents the details of an unplanned situation which has arisen, or is likely to arise, and records the proposed corrective action.

Records of Project Boards

Records of Project Boards provide accurate documentation of decisions made at Project Board meetings. These records document decisions and the rationale behind them and are not simply a set of minutes for the Project Board meetings. At each meeting, the record for the previous meeting should be agreed by the board members.

All major decisions and actions must be documented as the project progresses so that there is a complete historical record. Actions should be clear, personalised, unambiguous and time constrained.

The successive production of these records provides an audit trail of what has been accepted and of agreed commitments. This record helps to protect the relationship between the demand and supply organisations by establishing a point at which work and plans are accepted. The frequency of these points limits the necessity to back-track when problems arise. In this way, an element of project risk is controlled.

Checkpoint Reports	Checkpoint meetings are held as prescribed by the Project Controller on behalf of the Project Board. At each meeting, the Project Manager with help from the Project Assurance Team prepares a *Checkpoint Report* to summarise project progress. The Checkpoint Report is passed to the Project Controller.
Highlight Reports	*Highlight Reports* are prepared by the Project Manager at intervals determined by the Project Controller, on behalf of the Project Board, usually monthly. The Highlight Report contains a review of progress to date and highlights any problems which have been identified during the period covered.
Project Evaluation Report	The *Project Evaluation Report* (PER) is produced as part of the project closure process. The PER documents an assessment of the effectiveness of the management procedure used during the KBS development project. This information can then be used to ensure that the experience gained on this project is documented and can be used to improve procedures in future projects.
	The Project Evaluation Report is required as an input when there is to be a *post implementation review*. The post implementation review is concerned with evaluating whether the implemented system has delivered its perceived benefits and may look at several systems.
Progress Reports	*Progress Reports* are produced during the project lifetime to provide information to management. This information will be summarised in the final report.
	The personal progress reports of the project team are included within this category of products. These reports may be augmented by individual timesheets for the activities undertaken.

Chapter 4
Product Breakdown Structure

4.6 Technical Products Breakdown

The top-level of the Technical Products Breakdown contains the major products of the development process (See Figure 4.3).

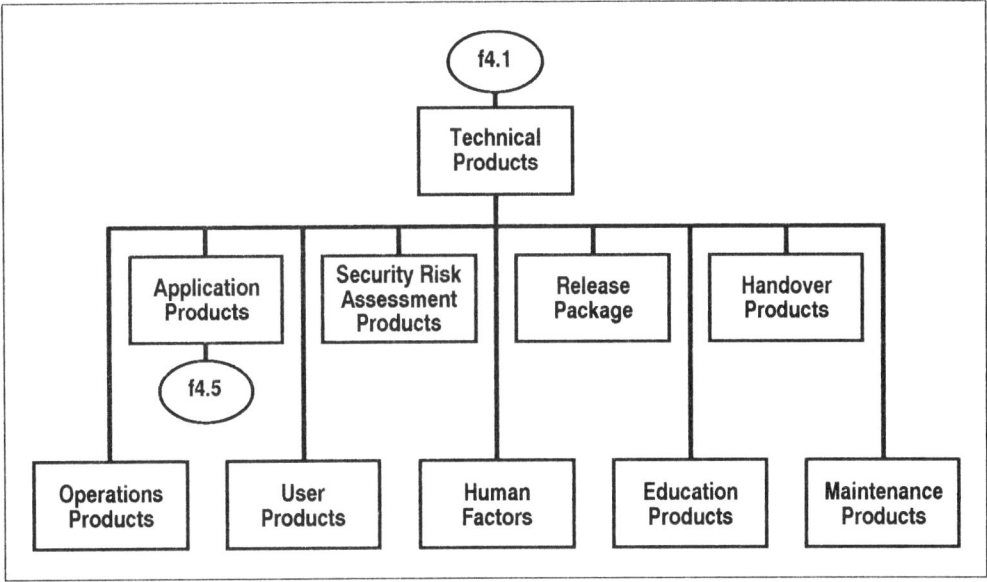

Figure 4.3: Technical Products Breakdown Structure

The PBS shows some Technical Products, which do not contribute directly to the developed KBS. These are products which are required to support development of an effective working final system. For example, Education Products are developed to ensure that everyone connected with the system receives appropriate training. Training is a necessary project activity which must be scheduled and resourced to achieve the project objectives.

Operations Products

Operations Products define the environment within which the applications are to run. These may be produced externally to the project or may already be in place. Nevertheless, they should be documented and subject to the same change control and configuration management procedures as other products in the project.

Products in this category include:

- capacity planning products
- hardware environment
- operating guide
- communications environment
- take-on data
- operating software
- application software
- operator training
- service level agreements.

The *operating guide* provides the operations staff with a description of the system, including full operating instructions and recovery procedures.

In this context, *data* is that which the implementation environment needs for processing. This data must be taken-on or converted from existing formats whether these are manually maintained documents or computer-based files.

The *Service Level Agreement* (SLA) is the definition of agreed (acceptable) levels of service. The document is agreed between the operations and user managements. A formal agreement may be signed after all parties are satisfied that the service levels are achievable, typically after three months of live running.

Application Products

Application Products are those normally associated with the development of the system. These include analysis, design and implementation products. These are described in section 4.8.

User Products

User Products provide the information that a user needs to be able to use the system. The User Guide explains how the system can be used and may act as both a training document and a reference manual. Information on issues such as siting of equipment may also be relevant here.

Chapter 4
Product Breakdown Structure

Security Risk Assessment Products

The *Security Risk Assessment Products* should be developed using a risk analysis method such as CCTA's CRAMM.

Steps can be taken to ensure that assets controlled by the system are safeguarded, by examining possible security risks and deciding what to do about them. The risks and counter-measures must be addressed within the requirements for the final system, so they need to be documented clearly and in a way appropriate for future use.

Human Factors Products

The *Human Factors Products* are used to prescribe ergonomic and job specification factors which need to be considered when designing systems.

These products should cover any aspect of the system which has an impact on people. This impact includes ergonomic information as well as details associated with a working application. Ideally, there will be overall standards set within an organisation. These standards need to be applied to each project and, where necessary, tailored to ensure that the specific user requirements can be met.

Education Products

Education Products are those necessary to teach the appropriate people how to work with the system. All the people concerned with the system must be considered for training, including:

- managers
- Knowledge Engineers
- designers
- developers
- implementers
- maintainers
- operators
- experts
- users.

An *Education Strategy* identifies the training which is required to run the system throughout its operational lifetime. This covers the training necessary to familiarise staff with the new system and may address future training needs.

The *Education Guide* describes how to train personnel so that they are able to manage, use, control, operate and maintain the new system. It includes instructions on how to use any educational software that has been developed.

Handover Products

Handover Products are those products which need to be passed on at the end of the project so that the system can continue to run and undergo change. This includes documentation about the system design and implementation as well as the Operations, User and Education Products already mentioned.

Release Package

The *Release Package* is the set of products which must be given to the operations staff so that a running system can be installed.

Maintenance Products

The *Maintenance Products* consist of documentation to support maintenance of the operational system. Maintenance of knowledge is a particular issue for KBS. Documentation needs to be provided to define who is responsible for identifying possible changes, where the new knowledge comes from and how control is exercised to prevent out-of-date knowledge being used.

4.7 Quality Products Breakdown

The *Quality Products* consist of a number of documents which are compiled as the project progresses. These products are used to show that quality control has been built into the project procedures and the implemented KBS (see Figure 4.4).

There are two other items of quality information which are documented as part of Management Products:

- quality assurance statement (QAS)
- quality plans.

Chapter 4
Product Breakdown Structure

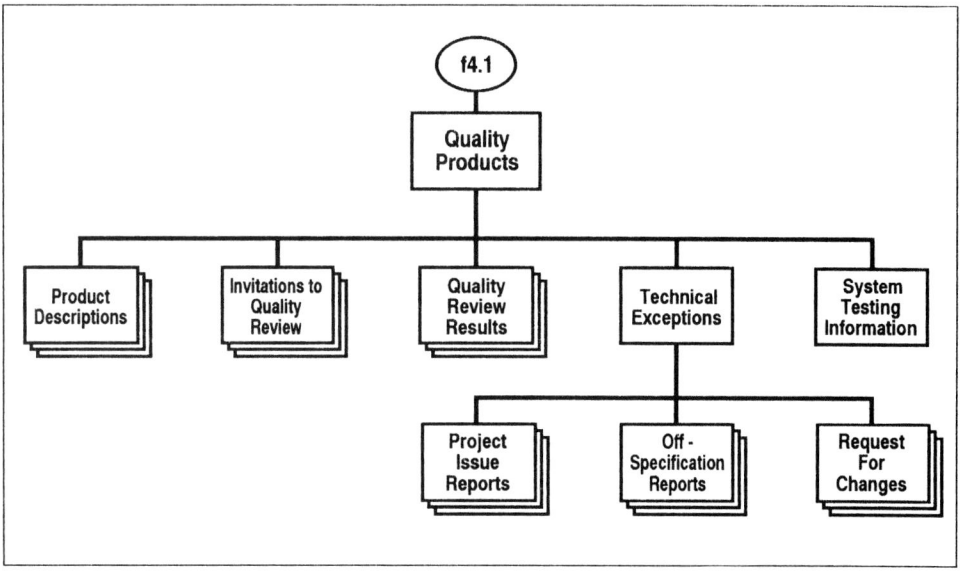

Figure 4.4: Quality Products Breakdown Structure

The *quality assurance statement* (QAS) documents the quality approach for the project. It is developed by the Project Controller to specify quality issues which must be addressed throughout the project. The approach is defined and documented at project initiation. This statement is referenced from, or included in, the Project Initiation Document.

Quality plans are a particular aspect of every plan but these may be documented individually if required for a particular project.

Product descriptions

Product descriptions are specified for all products of the project. The detail includes quality criteria against which the product can be checked to ensure that it is fit for purpose and of the required standard. Product descriptions are produced during planning and must be used during development to ensure products are developed according to plan.

Invitations to Quality Review	*Invitations to Quality Review* meetings confirm the date, time and, possibly, the format of the review with the reviewers, presenter(s) and a business representative.
Quality Review Results	*Quality Review Results* are sent to all attendees of the review meeting to notify them of the results of the review.
	The purpose of the Quality Review Results is to record and communicate the quality assessments of an independent quality review team. The content and structure of the reports is dictated by the quality plan. The quality assessments are carried out against the quality criteria in the relevant product description.
	These results should be communicated to the Project Board and the Project Controller, who use them as input to risk assessment.
Technical Exceptions	*Technical Exceptions* are used to highlight problems which have arisen during the lifetime of the project. There are three categories of exceptions to be documented, using the appropriate products:

- *Project Issue Reports* are used to document issues which relate to the project as a whole:

    - perceived errors and failures

    - inconsistencies between products

    - ideas for improvement and management issues

- *Off-Specification Reports* are used to document any situation where a product fails to meet its specification as laid down within the appropriate product description

- A *Request for Change* documents a request for modification to the system as currently planned; it does not imply that the change has been or will be implemented.

| System Testing Information | The *System Testing Information* includes a plan to show a schedule of the appropriate testing activities. The information should identify all the relevant types of testing of the project products, including component, system and user testing. Another component of this information is the detailed test data and associated expected results. |

4.8 Application Products Breakdown

Application Products are those Technical Products associated with the development of the system (See Figure 4.5).

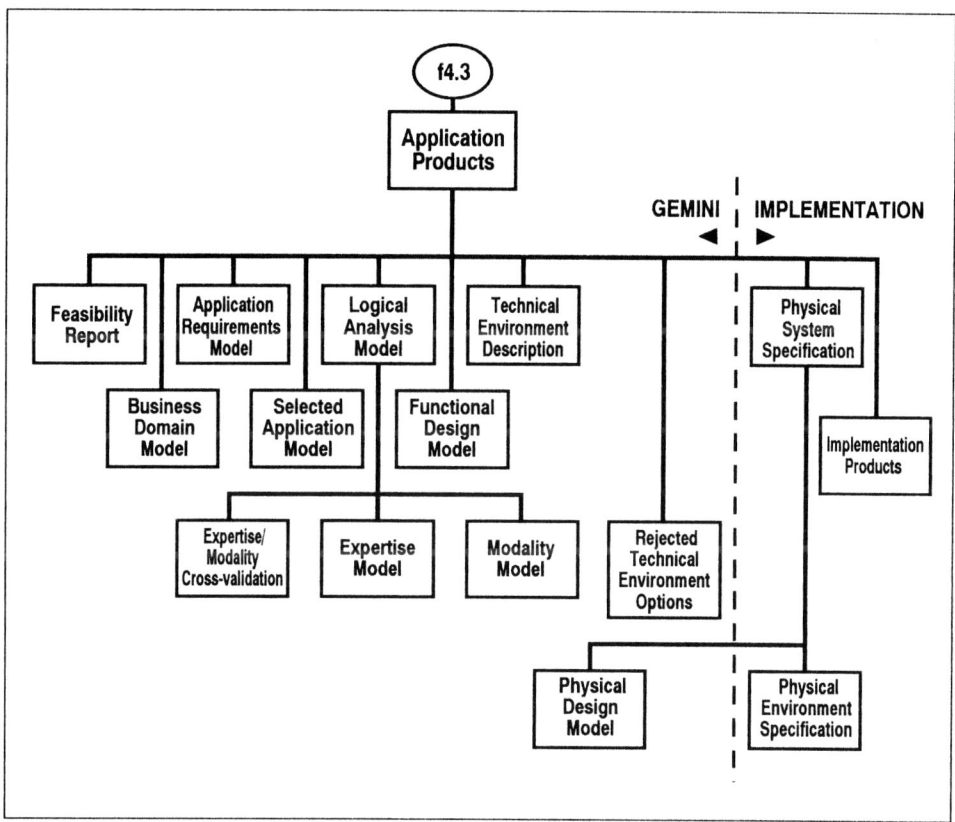

Figure 4.5: Application Products Breakdown Structure

These products include:

- the project documentation of the analysis and design activities, in this case GEMINI products
- the working physical system with its associated documentation.

A system is built by developing several products as shown in the above diagram. Each of these concentrates on a particular area of information.

Feasibility Report

The *Feasibility Report* records whether or not the users' needs can be reasonably met by the proposed system. There are three aspects to feasibility:

- business
- organisational
- technical.

Business Domain Model

The *Business Domain Model* is a representation of the organisational structure and business functions. The scope of potential applications may be identified based on this representation. The impact of a potential system on the organisation can be clarified and defined. For the potential applications the Business Domain Model covers both current and proposed systems and requirements.

Application Requirements Model

The *Application Requirements Model* holds a specification of the required external behaviour of the system, together with the organisational, operational, technical and resource constraints which affect the way that the system is to be designed and implemented.

Selected Application Model

The *Selected Application Model* is a representation of the tasks and data flows in an application. This representation provides a more precise definition of the functionality of the proposed application than the Business Domain Model.

Logical Analysis Model

The *Logical Analysis Model* is the pivotal product in a GEMINI-based project. It brings together the Expertise Model and the Modality Model into a single validated whole. The expert and user views of the application are drawn together and cross-validated to ensure that a coherent specification is built for the application. In addition to the Expertise Model and the Modality Model, the Logical Analysis Model contains documentation of the Expertise/Modality cross-validation.

The Logical Analysis Model forms the basis for the further design of the KBS. It is constructed before physical design constraints are considered. This means that the application knowledge within this model is defined in terms which are independent of the implementation environment.

The *Expertise Model* holds a description of the knowledge (expertise) to be encoded into the implemented KBS.

The *Modality Model* defines the agents in the proposed system and their way of interacting with each other. Agents are persons or other systems that interact with, or are components of, the proposed system. The Modality Model defines the agents, the tasks each performs and how they interact. It models when the agents can ask or give information. The pattern of interaction between agents is known as modality.

Functional Design Model

The *Functional Design Model* is a revision of the Logical Analysis Model. The revision reflects design decisions concerning how individual components of the system are to be implemented. For example, a rule-based approach may result in a very different functional design from an object-oriented approach.

The Functional Design Model is independent of any particular implementation environment. The model does not pre-empt the choice of features to be available in the hardware and software used for development and implementation of the operational KBS.

Technical Environment Description	The *Technical Environment Description* (TED) contains a definition of the requirements of the environment in which the application is to be developed and will run. The TED supports the Application Requirements Model by providing information on how the application requirements can be met. The information includes a description of the features that the hardware and software must support; for example if the user interface is to be based on windows. The features described include KBS and non-KBS elements. There must be information on system sizing, performance, data security and recovery, as the TED must provide sufficient information to support procurement.
Rejected Technical Environment Options	The *Rejected Technical Environment Options* provide management with documentation of the reasons why a particular approach to implementation is being advocated. This information can be used during the selection of the hardware and system software.
Physical System Specification	The *Physical System Specification* comprises the Physical Design Model and the Physical Environment Specification. The *Physical Design Model* provides a representation of all the components and functions of the system to be implemented. It is implementation dependent, the design details being dependent on the features of the chosen implementation environment. The *Physical Environment Specification* is a detailed description of the implementation environment. The information for this product is usually provided by the vendor.
Implementation Products	*Implementation Products* provide the detail necessary to set up the final working system, so that it adheres to the users' requirements. Much of the detail here is augmented by the Operations Products, User Products and Handover Products (see section 4.6).

4.9 Summary

In a KBS development project using GEMINI guidance, the Product Breakdown Structure shows how products progress the project from initial thoughts to final implementation of the system.

The three identified categories of product, while different, are complementary and all are needed to ensure that a high-quality solution is provided in a managed and controlled manner.

The spiral approach to managing a GEMINI-based project requires development of some Management Products which are additional to those identified within PRINCE. Development of these additional products manifests the GEMINI requirement for:

- continual assessment of risks to the project

- production of a workable solution within the given terms of reference. The terms of reference cover cost, time and resourcing of the development activities as well as identification of the benefits which will accrue from the implemented system.

Maintaining a complete set of products for a project provides information which can be used as the basis for implementation and to help with future maintenance. The products can also be used as a check on what was done in the project. Such a check can provide valuable information for future projects.

5 Product descriptions

5.1 Introduction

The information requirements for analysing and designing a knowledge based system application within GEMINI are defined in terms of products.

This chapter contains a definition of *product* and describes how a product needs to be defined within the context of GEMINI.

Subsequent sections of the chapter contain exemplar product descriptions for use within a GEMINI-based project. These exemplars should be used as a basis to create a full set of product descriptions, specific to each project and organisation.

Product

A *product* is any output from a project. The contents of a product must be sufficient to enable the product to fulfil its intended purpose within the project.

Some products are concerned purely with managing and controlling project activities. Other products focus on the technical information which must be drawn together to produce the necessary implemented system.

Product description

A *product description* contains details of the purpose, form and components of the product and a list of quality criteria which apply to it. The quality criteria are used to establish if the completed product is fit for its identified purpose.

Details of how and when the product is to be developed are specified in *activity descriptions* (see Chapters 6 and 7). Product and activity descriptions are used by management when estimating resource requirements and monitoring progress through the project.

5.2 Product description format

Product descriptions are required for each proposed product within the project. The product descriptions should be created and completed as far as possible during initial project planning. Early definition of the products aids accurate description and estimation of the work to be done.

Some GEMINI products will be passed from the supply-side to the demand-side. The Project Manager and Project Controller should agree product descriptions for these deliverables, before development is started. The users of the completed product may need to be involved with the process of reviewing and agreeing the product descriptions. Activity descriptions (see Chapter 7) provide information concerning who will undertake product development and the inputs required.

A product description has several sections which need to be completed. Each product description within this volume contains the following sections:

- name/identifier
- purpose
- composition/breakdown
- derivation
- quality, criteria and, if applicable, method
- external dependencies.

5.2.1 Name/identifier

Every product and component must have a *name* and an *identifier*.

Product names should be brief, unique and descriptive of the contents or purpose of the product as they may be used by non-technical people.

Product identifiers are used mainly by technical staff and may reflect a complex classification. The identifiers should be brief and must be unique. Products and their components should be consistently named and identified in all records available to an organisation.

There may be prescribed conventions for names and identifiers within an organisation. Compliance with any organisation standards is essential where they exist.

5.2.2 Purpose

Each product description includes a section which provides an explanation of why the product is required and may describe how it is to be used.

5.2.3 Composition and/or breakdown

Basic details of the required contents of the product should be defined. The characteristics of the product, other than quality or content, should be described, if they are necessary to convey a complete description of the product.

A diagram may be provided to show the structure of a product which is composed of several other products. This diagram is used to show how the individual components fit together to make up the whole product.

A small product can reasonably be described as a report, a form or a document. Standards of layout and presentation may be incorporated or cross-referenced for large products. A description of the technology to be used to create the product may be included.

Care must be taken not to break products down to too low a level. The potential for separate development should be used to determine what are discrete components of products. A component must not be further broken down if the production of the component could not be similarly broken down.

5.2.4 Derivation

The information required to develop the product should be identified.

5.2.5 Quality

The quality of an individual product is determined by the quality criteria to which it is developed, together with the processes and techniques used to develop it. Factors that affect product quality are documented in one of three ways as follows:

- as quality criteria on a product description
- as tasks within the work structure
- as detail within the development technique.

The first factor is properly part of the product description and is dealt with below. The others concern development activities and are documented in activity descriptions, with any relevant information referenced in the product description .

There are two specific aspects to the quality section of a product description:

- criteria - against which quality is assessed
- method - used for assessing the product and signing it off when it is of an acceptable standard.

Quality criteria

In general, the quality criteria documented in this section are applied during development of the product. These quality criteria are also used as checks in the product quality reviews to validate products for completeness and consistency.

An individual product may be a component of another product, have another product as a component or be interdependent with another product. This can give problems where some aspects of a review could involve reviewing a separate product. These problems can be addressed by ensuring that quality criteria for such aspects are set at the appropriate product level, which is the lowest level common to the interdependency.

	Standard quality criteria	Some quality criteria must be applied whenever documentation is being produced. These criteria tend to be common sense and should be applied to the product during development and on review. The criteria include:

- appropriate content in terms of detail and presentation
- clarity, accuracy and consistency of statements conveying the required message
- purpose fulfilled by product
- use of language, including correct spelling, grammar, and punctuation
- conformance to specific installation standards; issues covered here include style and presentation.

These standard quality criteria have not been reiterated throughout the product descriptions. It is assumed that an installation would have a standard procedure for applying criteria of this nature.

	Method of quality review	Within the quality section of the product description, it is possible to state what method of review is required, generally *formal* or *informal*. All products should be subject to informal reviews. All deliverables and all products used for Project Board decisions must be formally reviewed. Where formal review is essential, this is indicated in the quality section.

Guidance on conducting a review is given in *GEMINI: Controlling KBS Development Projects*.

5.2.6 External dependencies

Not all products can be developed from within the GEMINI-based project. Some products require input from sources external to the project or the project organisation skill base, for example, individuals with particular skills, such as capacity planners or legal experts. These external dependencies must be identified and listed.

5.3 Described products

There are many products developed within a project. This volume concentrates on GEMINI-specific products, including products that occur, with different content, in a conventional development project.

Definitive description of a product depends on the methods and techniques used to develop the product. GEMINI does not prescribe which techniques to employ, as the factors affecting the applicability of techniques are project-dependent. Chapter 8 describes some relevant techniques and section 8.6 relates these to each of the main Application Products.

The exemplar product descriptions given in the following sections are intended as initial outlines of the content appropriate to the products. For any particular project, each product description must be tailored to comply with installation standards as well as to reflect the requirements for the project.

The following products are described:

Product	*Section*
Activity description	5.4
Application Requirements Model	5.5
Business Domain Model	5.6
Circuit Initiation Document	5.7
Expertise Model	5.8
Feasibility Report	5.9
Functional Design Model	5.10
Logical Analysis Model	5.11
Management Risk Assessment	5.12
Modality Model	5.13
Physical Design Model	5.14

Chapter 5
Product descriptions

Product	Section
Physical Environment Specification	5.15
Physical System Specification	5.16
Plan	5.17
Product Breakdown Structure	5.18
Product description	5.19
Product Flow Diagram	5.20
Progress Report	5.21
Project Initiation Document	5.22
Rejected Technical Environment Options	5.23
Selected Application Model	5.24
Technical Environment Description	5.25
Technical Environment Options	5.26
Work structure	5.27

5.4 Activity description

5.4.1 Purpose

The purpose of an activity description is to define the tasks which must be undertaken so that the necessary products can be developed during the lifetime of the project.

Each activity description defines the tasks textually, but precisely and formally. Each defines and explains the sequence and dependencies of what is to be produced and how it is to be produced. The participants are identified, that is, those who should undertake the task or the skill levels required. The activities are defined as a hierarchy of other activities.

Chapter 6 defines the main activities required in a GEMINI development project.

Chapter 7 includes exemplar activity descriptions for a GEMINI-based project.

5.4.2 Composition

The following information should be included for each activity description as required:

- heading details
- activity details.

Heading details

For each activity description, the heading details must provide a unique identifier within a particular project:

- activity description identifier
- activity name
- level in the activity hierarchy.

Activity details

Activity details consist of several elements of information. Not all of these elements may be required for every activity. The required information includes:

- objective
- summary
- participants
- preconditions:
    - management authorisation
    - inputs
    - reference material
- products
- techniques
- activities which make up this one.

5.4.3 Derivation

Activity descriptions are derived from:

- installation standards for production management
- GEMINI exemplar activity descriptions
- details of the required products
- techniques to be used for product development.

5.4.4 Quality   Activity descriptions are produced during planning.

       Criteria   The activity description quality criteria include:

For each:

- does the activity have a name, level identifier, objective, participant and product?
- are references to products and product components correct and accurate?
- is the management level responsible for authorisation identified and appropriate, taking into account product interdependencies?

For the set:

- are all the project activities described?
- are any interdependencies and cross-references clearly documented?
- are all necessary project products developed within the complete set of activities?

5.4.5 External dependencies   The external dependencies of activity descriptions vary in accordance with:

- the activity covered
- project specific issues.

Chapter 5
Product descriptions
Activity description

5.5 Application Requirements Model

5.5.1 Purpose

The purpose of an Application Requirements Model is to establish an understanding of user requirements and give a firm basis to scope the application.

This product brings together the various requirements lists. Its purpose is to allow an overview of all requirements, making conflicts and redundancies more visible at a glance.

The Application Requirements Model holds a specification of the required external behaviour of the system, together with the organisational, operational, technical and resource constraints which affect the way that the system is to be defined and implemented. It is important to express requirements concerning the maintenance of the system.

The role of this product is the same as that of user requirements in conventional system development.

5.5.2 Composition

The Application Requirements Model contains structured, prioritised lists of requirements.

All requirements listed must be designated *mandatory* or *desirable*. Desirable requirements may also be assigned priorities according to their desirability.

The lists must cover requirements from several perspectives, namely business, organisational, management, technical, system, user, training, development, maintenance, delivery, external interface and project including policy.

Requirements, taking into account all these perspectives, can be grouped into four environments to enable the project to move from the current situation to the required situation:

- operating environment
- development environment
- transition environment
- project environment.

Operating environment	The requirements of the *operating environment* of the delivered (implemented) system include:

- functional requirements of the system to be developed
- non-functional requirements of the system to be developed
- staff roles
- organisational structure
- security and integrity constraints
- legal requirements
- audit requirements
- operational costs. |
| Development environment | The requirements of the *development environment* for producing the system, taking care that decisions taken now do not pre-empt later decisions on the operating environment, include:

- types of software and hardware to be used for development
- technical expertise relating to development
- application domain expertise
- development budget and timescales. |
| Transition environment | The *transition environment* is concerned with the issues of implementing the developed system, taking account of the current systems and policies. The requirements of the organisation for the transition environment depend on:

- current software and hardware policies
- future software and hardware policies
- implementation budget and timescales
- departmental organisation and phasing-in issues
- data transfer issues. |

	Project environment	The requirements of the *project environment* for successful completion include:

- resource constraints
- quality constraints
- project policy constraints. |
| 5.5.3 | Derivation | The Application Requirements Model is derived from:

- the Project Initiation Document
- documentation of existing systems
- interviews with users and experts. |
| 5.5.4 | Quality | The outline Application Requirements Model is created during Feasibility Study and developed in Requirements Analysis, System modelling, Logical Analysis and Technical Environment Definition. The output from each of these activities will be a version of the model forming a discrete product. The product description for each of these versions will build on any existing product description. |
| | Criteria | The Application Requirements Model quality criteria will depend on the activity developing it, but will include the following:

- are there any conflicting requirements?
- are the requirements consistent with the organisation's IS strategy?
- are the requirements consistent with the project terms of reference as laid down in the Project Initiation Document?
- are the requirements consistent with the overall business objectives for the organisation? |

- is each requirement described in sufficient detail to form the basis for decisions relating to the suitability of the application for implementation?

- do requirements relating to the performance of the delivered system include measurable targets, for example, response time or accuracy of the system advice?

- have future operation and maintenance of the system been adequately reflected in the requirements?

- where requirements have been brought forward from previous versions of the model, are they consistent? If not, why has the inconsistency arisen?

- have any requirements been eliminated from previous versions of the model? If so, were they excluded for adequate reasons?

- have all requirements got source, owner, priority and benefit defined?

5.5.5 External dependencies

The external dependencies of the Application Requirements Model may include:

- organisation and management skills
- security expertise
- audit expertise
- project-specific dependencies
- activity-specific dependencies
- commitment of management to provide the resources to define the requirements.

5.6 Business Domain Model

5.6.1 Purpose

The purpose of a Business Domain Model is to provide a representation of the enterprise, giving an understanding of the organisational structure and business function. There is a significant amount of information about the enterprise which is entirely independent of any selected application.

From this view of the business, the scope of possible applications may be identified. The impact of a potential system on the organisation can be clarified and defined. For the potential applications, the Business Domain Model covers both current and proposed systems and requirements.

5.6.2 Composition

The Business Domain Model includes a sketch of the business within which the system will be sited, covering:

- business structure
- business objectives
- business problems.

as well as a set of outline application profiles, each having an initial set of requirements and assessment of feasibility.

5.6.3 Derivation

The Business Domain Model is derived from:

- analysis of the business
- strategy studies
- interviews with management
- Project Initiation Document.

5.6.4 Quality

The outline Business Domain Model is created during Feasibility Study, then developed in Requirements Analysis and System Modelling. The output from each of these activities will be a version of the model, forming a discrete product. The product description for each of these versions will build on any existing product descriptions.

Criteria

The Business Domain Model quality criteria include:

- are there any conflicting objectives?
- is the information consistent with the organisation's IS strategy?
- is the information consistent with the business objectives?
- is each application described in sufficient detail to provide an initial assessment of feasibility?

5.6.5 External dependencies

The external dependencies of the Business Domain Model include:

- availability of management for interviews
- information on the organisation's business strategy
- a global view of the organisation.

5.7 Circuit Initiation Document (CID)

5.7.1 Purpose

The purpose of the Circuit Initiation Document is to gather together the information needed to control the work which is to be undertaken during a circuit of the spiral. This information includes defining the objectives and boundaries of the activities. The CID is the mechanism for conveying this information to the project team.

The information in the CID must be within the project boundary as set out in the PID and consistent with it. The latest CID forms the current project baseline and scopes the next circuit of the spiral. These details are an update of the previous baseline which was set in the PID or previous Circuit Initiation Documents. In this context, the CID is used during the next review phase to assess the progress which has been made in the current spiral circuit.

The CID for the following circuit of the spiral model is developed at the end of each review process. Management approval of this product is required before the next circuit of the spiral can commence.

5.7.2 Composition

In general, this document is a cut down version of the PID. The CID incorporates detailed information relevant to the next set of development activities as well as overall plans for the rest of the project.

Sections of the CID cover:

- aims and objectives
- project boundary
- functional definition
- quality assurance statement
- project organisation.

See the product description for a Product Initiation Document, for further details.

5.7.3	Derivation	The Circuit initiation Document is derived from:

- the current Management Risk Assessment
- the Project Initiation Document
- the previous Circuit Initiation Document
- Progress Reports.

5.7.4	Quality	A CID is developed during each review sector for use in the next circuit of the spiral.
	Criteria	The CID quality criteria include the following:

- is the composition as stated in the product description?
- are the names of personnel shown against the roles required?
- have the people named agreed to act and to commit the time as scheduled?
- have dates been set for all the control meetings and reports?
- have measures been proposed for all the risks identified for the project?
- have the Project Plans been reviewed and agreed?
- does the CID fit within the terms of reference as laid down in the Project Initiation Document?

	Method	Formal review before submission to the relevant management level for approval.
5.7.5	External dependencies	Any external dependencies of the CID will be project specific.

5.8 Expertise Model

5.8.1 Purpose

The purpose of an Expertise Model is to draw together information which is necessary for the application to support the required functionality. The Expertise Model portrays the specialist (expert) information for the application in a structured form.

5.8.2 Composition

There are four basic interrelated components of information which need to be drawn together in the Expertise Model:

- strategic knowledge
- tactical knowledge
- inference knowledge
- domain data.

Some example representations are given below. More detail on these can be found in Chapter 8.

Strategic knowledge

Strategic knowledge specifies how the system plans a way out of a task impasse and how it can schedule different tasks. Part of the focus is to ensure efficient use of resources when scheduling tasks.

Strategic knowledge allows conflict resolution between competing or complementary tasks.

The strategic knowledge provides a specification of how the tactical knowledge is to be used. Supporting information is supplied by the inference knowledge.

Example representations:

- diagrammatic models
- First Order Predicate Logic
- structured English.

Tactical knowledge
: *Tactical knowledge* describes the sequences in which the *inference knowledge* can be used.

Different ways in which a task can be performed are relevant here. This aspect covers identification and description of possible task execution sequences.

Example representations:

- structured English
- extended dataflow models
- descriptive prose.

Inference knowledge
: *Inference knowledge* provides a description of the reasoning process to be performed, with links to items defined in the *domain data*.

The inference knowledge is the underlying logic which has to be applied to the domain data to solve a particular problem.

Example representations:

- diagrammatic models
- structured English
- Production Rules.

Domain data
: *Domain data* consists of the key information necessary for the application to carry out the required tasks. The domain data are likely to be described in terms of facts, concepts and relationships pertinent to the application.

The domain data is used by inference knowledge and tactical knowledge to enable the KBS to perform the required function.

Example representations:

- semantic nets
- extended Logical Data Models
- Frames.

5.8.3 Derivation

The Expertise Model is derived primarily from interviews with experts. Also from:

- Selected Application Model
- Application Requirements Model
- Business Domain Model.

5.8.4 Quality

The Expertise Model is developed in the Logical Analysis activity.

Criteria

The Expertise Model quality criteria include:

- are each of the four components consistent?
- is each piece of knowledge allocated a source, owner and requirement to which it relates?
- is any knowledge redundant?
- is any knowledge inaccessible? For example, data not manipulated by anything or tactical knowledge that can never be activated
- are all diagrams syntactically correct?

5.8.5 External dependencies

The external dependencies of the Expertise Model include:

- management commitment to resolve conflicts between experts
- project specific dependencies.

Chapter 5
Product descriptions
Expertise Model

5.9 Feasibility Report

5.9.1 Purpose

The purpose of the Feasibility Report is:

- to address the business, organisational and technical feasibility of the project
- to record management decisions about the options for further work, including whether a proposed information system should be cancelled, re-scoped, split or merged with another
- to form the basis of the case for management to commit the resources for a Full Study
- to provide a supporting document for the application to proceed
- to provide information for each Full Study, as a record of decisions, assumptions, estimates, user requirements and outline options
- to provide an outline plan for managing each Full Study
- to record the findings of the Feasibility Study team according to the terms of reference agreed at the start of the study
- to document the work done in the Feasibility Study and provide evidence to justify the findings.

5.9.2 Composition

The report has ten sections which require completion. Any information of a highly technical nature which is required to support the main body of the report should be included in the Annexes.

Chapter 5
Product descriptions
Feasibility Report

Introduction	The Introduction provides details of the following:
	• reason for the study
	• terms of reference for the study
	• study objectives
	• scope of the study
	• constraints
	• completion date
	• consultation
	• management of the study.
Management summary	The management or executive summary includes brief details of:
	• the recommended solution
	• the options considered but rejected
	• the plans for the Full Study
	• the preferred procurement path
	• the plans for the implementation of the system.
Study approach	This section details how the study was conducted and its cost.
Existing business and its IS support	This section documents the current situation in the area under study, detailing:
	• the business objectives
	• the functions and processes that are currently undertaken
	• the organisation of the business area, and the various roles and responsibilities
	• the current and potential areas of strength and weakness

- any relationships with other business areas and organisations
- any existing IS support detailing the functions supported or not:
  - strengths and weaknesses
  - technological opportunities
  - constraints.

Where appropriate, the suitability of knowledge-based systems technology to an application may be stated.

Future required IS

Future IS support required by the business includes details of:

- a description of the system's place in the IS Strategy
- an overview of the scope of the required system and its functionality
- details of the requirements, expressed in measurable terms
- the requirements for and implications of any geographic distribution of IS support
- details of the service performance required of the proposed system.

Proposed system

Proposed system section describes how the above requirements can be met, including:

- a narrative overview of the logical system, based on the findings
- an outline of the alternative technological options, together with a summary of the necessary technical approach
- the advantages and disadvantages of the team's proposals.

Rejected options	All of the options which were considered during the Feasibility Study should be described in a similar manner to the proposed system but in less detail, highlighting the reasons for non-selection.
Financial assessment	The financial assessment gives a summary of the estimated costs of the proposed system, comparing the proposed system with other options and summarising benefits against current weaknesses.
Project Plan	This section gives an outline Project Plan for any proposed course of action. The plan includes resource requirements and expected implementation timescale and outlines the management structure for the development and implementation exercises.
Conclusions	This section documents the study conclusions and the resulting recommendations.
Annexes	The annexes provide supporting documentation for the items within the main body of the report, including documentation of the appropriate initial technical products.

5.9.3 Derivation

The Feasibility Report is derived from:

- the organisation's IS strategy
- *terms of reference* within the Project Initiation Document
- interviews with experts and users.

5.9.4 Quality   The Feasibility Report is developed in the Feasibility Study activity.

Criteria   The Feasibility Report quality criteria include:

For Management and user acceptance:

- does the Feasibility Report:
    - conform to installation standards?
    - accord with the IS Strategy?
    - conform to the project terms of reference as stated in the Project Initiation Document?
- is the proposed solution within the identified budget constraints?
- is the project within the scope set? Can it continue based on this scope?
- do the users agree that their requirements have been addressed?

For technical assessment:

- is one and only one option selected as the way ahead? This option may be a combination of aspects from several of the suggested options
- are all the requirements mutually consistent? If not, have priorities been identified?
- is it an accurate statement of requirements, constraints and possible future enhancements to the system?

Method   Formal review of this product is required prior to management acceptance.

5.9.5 External dependencies

The external dependencies of the Feasibility Report are organisation and project specific. They may include:

- availability of experts and users to participate in selecting the recommended way forward, if appropriate

- availability of the management team to conduct the review.

5.10 Functional Design Model

5.10.1 Purpose

The purpose of a Functional Design Model is to communicate high-level design options to the appropriate level of management for approval.

This product reflects design decisions concerning how individual components of the system will be implemented. The Functional Design Model should be independent of any particular implementation environment. The model should not pre-empt the choice of features to be available in the hardware and software used in the operational system.

5.10.2 Composition

The composition of the Functional Design Model is dependent on the technique chosen to develop it (see Chapter 8). The techniques are likely to be diagrammatic.

5.10.3 Derivation

The Functional Design Model is derived primarily from the Logical Analysis Model with input from the Selected Application Model and the Application Requirements Model.

5.10.4 Quality

The Functional Design Model is developed in the Logical Design activity.

Criteria

The Functional Design Model quality criteria include:

- is the design independent of any specific implementation?
- are all reasonable options identified and discussed?
- are all functions linked back to the Logical Analysis Model?
- are all functions linked back to requirements?

- is the product sufficiently detailed for definition of a suitable technical environment?
- is the product sufficiently detailed for Physical Design activities to proceed once the technical environment has been chosen?

5.10.5 External dependencies

The external dependencies of the Functional Design Model include:

- availability of capacity planners
- knowledge of the techniques to be used
- knowledge of the restrictions that the techniques may place on the physical implementation.

5.11 Logical Analysis Model

5.11.1 Purpose

The purpose of a Logical Analysis Model is to bring the Modality Model and Expertise Model together into a single consistent and validated whole.

The expert and user views of the application are drawn together and the individual components cross-validated to ensure that a coherent specification is built for the application.

The Logical Analysis Model forms the basis for the further design of the implementable system. It is constructed before physical design constraints are considered, which means that within this model the application knowledge is defined in terms which are independent of the implementation environment.

5.11.2 Composition

The Logical Analysis Model consists of:

- Expertise Model (section 5.8)
- Modality Model (section 5.13)
- Expertise/Modality Cross-validation.

The third element provides cross-referencing between the elements of the two models.

5.11.3 Derivation

The Logical Analysis Model is derived from:

- Expertise Model
- Modality Model
- interviews with experts and users.

5.11.4 Quality

The Logical Analysis Model is developed in the Logical Analysis activity.

Criteria

The Logical Analysis Model quality criteria include:

- are all parts of the Logical Analysis Model consistent?
- are Modality Model entities validated against Expertise Model domain data?
- are Modality Model tasks validated against Expertise Model inference knowledge?
- are Modality Model task plans validated against Expertise Model tactical knowledge?
- are task projections validated against Expertise Model strategic knowledge?
- is the cross-validation between Expertise Model and Modality Model adequately documented?
- is the Logical Analysis Model consistent with its constituent models?
- is sufficient detail provided to proceed to logical design?

5.11.5 External dependencies

The external dependencies of a Logical Analysis Model include management commitment to resolve conflicts between user and expert views of the application.

5.12 Management Risk Assessment

5.12.1 Purpose

The purpose of the Management Risk Assessment product is to detail the risk assessment undertaken for management during the risk assessment sector of a circuit of the spiral model. Management Risk Assessment should contain information at a sufficient level of detail to allow reassessment of feasibility and reappraisal of project objectives.

The product must identify those areas of the project which affect the likelihood that the project can be completed on time and within budget. The product must include a recommendation of the option to be taken to mitigate the identified risks.

5.12.2 Composition

The product incorporates:

- risk identification and quantification
- resolution options.

Exception Plans may be appended to show how particular resolution options can be resourced and scheduled.

Risk identification and quantification

A comprehensive list of quantified potential risks between now and successful project completion in order of seriousness. Risks are compared and quantified according to:

- the likelihood of the risk becoming actual (probability)
- the consequences of the risk becoming actual (severity).

The importance of the risk in relation to other risks (relative priority) should be identified.

This part of the product is, in effect, a record of the assumptions underlying the current plan.

Chapter 5
Product descriptions
Management Risk Assessment

Resolution options	An outline of strategies and tactics for managing the risks, business, organisational and technical, associated with specified options. This detail must cover any impact on other risks caused by addressing each risk. Criteria of risk acceptability and unacceptability must be specified. Options other than least risk will be judged, retrospectively, in the light of these criteria.

This section also includes the proposed way ahead for the project.

5.12.3 Derivation

Each Management Risk Assessment is derived from:

- Project Initiation Document
- Circuit Initiation Document
- Feasibility Report
- previous Management Risk Assessments
- Risk management issues (Annex A).

5.12.4 Quality

The Management Risk Assessment is developed in the risk assessment sector of the spiral.

Criteria

The Management Risk Assessment quality criteria include the following:

- is the list of risks complete?
- are there separate assessments of probability and severity?
- are the risks sufficiently specific?
- are the resolution options relevant and feasible?
- are the resolution options explained in sufficient detail? Are the effects stated? Do they address both probability and severity?

- are the resolution options sufficient? Are there valid options not considered? Are there any superfluous options to give the appearance of choice?

- are any of the risks or resolution options interrelated? If so, are the impacts identified adequately?

- will the options have the result stated?

- are the options that require approval from the Project Board highlighted?

- is the correct option selected?

- do any of the options require project objectives to be reconsidered? If so is this highlighted.

- has the continued viability of the project been assessed?

5.12.5 External dependencies

The main external dependency of a Management Risk Assessment is the availability of risk assessment expertise within the appropriate areas including:

- business organisation
- IT security
- legal issues.

Chapter 5
Product descriptions
Management Risk Assessment

5.13 Modality Model

5.13.1 Purpose

The purpose of the Modality Model is to define the interactions in the proposed operational system. Agents are persons or processes that interact with or are components of the final system. The Modality Model provides a definition of which agents perform which tasks and how the agents interact. It also covers the circumstances where the agents can ask for or give information. The pattern of interaction between agents is known as modality.

This product is used to ensure that user requirements and technical interface possibilities are evaluated concurrently and that tasks are allocated to agents effectively.

This is a critical product for the usability of the system and is important in managing the users' expectation of the system and providing a guide to interface design issues.

5.13.2 Composition

There are several aspects to the Modality Model as follows:

- task model
- list of agents
- allocation of tasks to agents
- interaction model.

Task model

Bubble chart or block diagram of hierarchical tasks supplemented by:

- descriptions of data (entities)
- indications of dataflow
- taskplans for traversing the chart
- objectives of tasks
- detail of tasks.

List of agents	Agents that can instigate or perform tasks.
Allocation of agents to tasks	Documentation of which agents are involved with which tasks and the nature of the dialogues.
Interaction model	How the tasks and agents interact.

5.13.3 Derivation

The Modality Model is derived from:

- Interviews with users
- Application Requirements Model
- Selected Application Model
- Business Domain Model.

5.13.4 Quality

The Modality Model is developed in the Logical Analysis activity.

Criteria

The Modality Model quality criteria include:

- are all agents identified?
- are all tasks allocated to agents?
- are the tasks broken down to a reasonable level?
- are the flows of data between tasks identified?
- are the events that trigger tasks identified?
- is the information passed between agents identified and consistent with the flows of data between tasks?
- is the instigator identified for agents and tasks?
- are the diagrams syntactically correct?
- are objectives identified for the agents? Are the objectives genuine problem solving requirements?

5.13.5 External dependencies

The main external dependency of the Modality Model is the commitment of management to resolve any conflict between users as to the nature of the requirements.

Chapter 5
Product descriptions
Modality Model

5.14 Physical Design Model

5.14.1 Purpose

The purpose of a Physical Design Model is to record details of how the application functionality, as documented in the Functional Design Model, is to be implemented within the chosen technical environment.

The Physical Design Model provides a representation of all the components and functions of the system to be implemented. It is implementation dependent, the design details being dependent on the technical environment chosen for implementation. The Physical Design Model will reflect the features of the generic types of hardware and software to be used. If the actual items have been chosen, specific features of these may be taken into account.

The product provides a record of the types of functions which need to be implemented and matches these function types to techniques applicable to their implementation.

5.14.2 Composition

There are several elements to the Physical Design Model. These include specifications of the information content (knowledge base), the processing requirements and the system interface. The form of these specifications will depend on the techniques chosen to develop the Physical Design Model. Example forms are:

- diagrammatic, for example, state transition diagrams
- descriptive text, structured english, pseudo-code
- software prototypes for screen layouts.

5.14.3 Derivation

The Physical Design Model is derived from:

- Functional Design Model
- Application Requirements Model
- Physical Environment Specification.

5.14.4 Quality

Criteria

The Physical Design Model quality criteria include:

- are the processing aspects identified and defined clearly?
- will the system work in a way that will support the users, as required?
- are all the tasks in the Functional Design Model encompassed by the Physical Design Model?
- is the design feasible within the chosen technical environment?
- are the processing and knowledge elements consistent and complete?
- are the processing requirements specified in a form which is suitable for the chosen implementation environment?
- is the development environment compatible with the implementation requirement?

5.14.5 External dependencies

The external dependencies of the Physical Design Model include:

- understanding of the implementation vehicle by the development team
- availability of the skills required to develop it
- project specification dependencies.

5.15 Physical Environment Specification

5.15.1 Purpose

The purpose of a Physical Environment Specification is to specify the hardware and software products and the services required to implement an operational KBS. This product includes details of the configuration to be supplied, commissioned and made available for implementation.

Notes:

1 The Physical Environment Specification may identify different products or configurations for development and operational systems

2 The Physical Environment Specification may include a range of products in a distributed environment.

5.15.2 Composition

The Physical Environment Specification is composed of descriptions of:

- all hardware products and versions to be supplied

- all software products and versions to be supplied including DBMS, application generator, TPMS, operating system, networking support, KBS tools, programming languages, application packages

- hardware configuration

- software configuration

- operating documentation

- reference manuals

- licensing arrangements

- policy covering the upgrading of any software

- maintenance arrangements for hardware and software.

Chapter 5
Product descriptions
Physical Environmental Specification

The detailed composition will depend on installation standards. It must be suitable for the demand side to use to judge the viability of an IS-provider's offering.

5.15.3 Derivation

Generally provided by an external supplier from the Technical Environment Description (section 5.25).

5.15.4 Quality

Criteria

The Physical Environment Specification quality criteria include:

- is the format and content as required?
- does this product adhere to installation standards?
- are all facets of the Technical Environment Description covered? If not is their omission allowable?

5.15.5 External dependencies

The external dependencies of the Physical Environment Specification include:

- supplier's ability to provide the technical environment information in a suitable format
- project specific dependencies.

5.16 Physical System Specification

5.16.1 Purpose

The purpose of a Physical System Specification is to define an operationally viable system to meet the system requirements, consistent with the Functional Design Model. This will give management sufficient information to agree a way ahead.

This product combines the Physical Design Model with the Physical Environment Specification to define the actual implementation environment.

5.16.2 Composition

This product has two components which are described in more detail within this set of product descriptions. The relevant products are:

- Physical Design Model (section 5.14)
- Physical Environment Specification (section 5.15)
- cross validation information to show how the supplies and services in the Physical Environment Specification match the functions in the Physical Design Model.

Any project or installation standards should be taken into account.

5.16.3 Derivation

The Physical System Specification is produced by combining the Physical Design Model and Physical Environment Specification.

5.16.4 Quality

Criteria

The Physical System Specification quality criteria include:

For Management and user acceptance:

- does the specification conform to installation standards? That is, does it fit into the technical policies of the IS Strategy and conform to the terms of reference as laid down in the Project Initiation Document (PID)?

- are project budget and resources within the scope set in the PID?

- do the users agree that this solution addresses their requirements?

- can the project continue to the construction and testing phase?

For Technical assurance:

- is the specification viable and implementable?

- does the Physical Environment Specification component agree with the Technical Environment Description

- does the specification take account of hardware/software limitations for development and implementation? That is, is there consistency between the Physical Design Model and the Physical Environment Specification?

- are appropriate migration paths identified if the development and implementation environments differ?

- are maintenance issues addressed satisfactorily?

- does the specification achieve a satisfactory balance between performance and functionality? Have any resource implications for development, testing, operation and maintenance been assessed?
- do all aspects of user interface, that is menus, screens, reports, user and operating manuals meet requirements?
- do the detailed processes of the system:
    - provide all required functionality?
    - meet system performance requirements?
    - make acceptable demands on human or material resources?
    - have acceptable hardware requirements?
    - conform to operations/management rules?
- have acceptance criteria been defined?
- has the likely impact, of the system specified, on the users, been identified?

Method — Formal review

5.16.5 External dependencies

The external dependencies of the physical system Specification include:

- management commitment to allow changes to the requirements which are necessary to produce an effective implementable design
- management commitment to adopt procedures required to enable the system to be implemented and operated
- project specific dependencies.

Chapter 5
Product descriptions
Physical System Specification

5.17 Plan

5.17.1 Purpose

The purpose of a plan is to provide identification of the products which must be developed during the project or next development sector of the spiral model. There must be a specification of the activities needed to develop the identified products. A plan should provide a specification of how quality of the products will be assured as well as identifying the resources needed for quality control.

A plan shows the products, activities and resources required on a project or on an activity within a project. The plan forms an agreed baseline for the resource and scheduling requirements for the activities covered.

All plans are updated with actual resource usage as a project proceeds. The initial Project Plan forms a baseline which is the major reference for management to monitor the progress of activities throughout the project.

There are three types of Plan:

- Project Plan
- Development Sector Plan
- Exception Plan.

The *Project Plan* sets out the overall approach which is to be taken on the project. The products and activities covered will be major ones.

A *Development Sector Plan* documents and schedules the resources required to develop the Technical Products covered by one circuit of the spiral.

An *Exception Plan* documents an unplanned situation that has arisen and records proposed corrective action.

5.17.2 Composition

Format and presentation will be in accordance with the organisation's or the site's standards. Plans will include some narrative of what is detailed and include an explanation of reasons for inclusion or exclusion of activities. Each Plan should include technical, resource and quality aspects.

Technical plan

A technical plan shows the products to be developed and target completion dates given (elapsed timescales). Identified tolerances must be shown. Managers in charge of the development of the products will be identified. Dependencies between the project and other projects should be identified.

Technical plans may be documented by use of any of the following:

- Product Breakdown Structure supported by product descriptions
- Product Flow Diagram
- activity network or work structure supported by activity descriptions
- barchart
- graphical summary.

Resource plans

A resource plan shows estimates of amounts of each resource type required during each time period (predefined, may be monthly, weekly). These estimates should be based on the detail in the technical and quality plans.

Resource plans include the resourcing requirements for each activity and the whole project, including control tolerance details for the project.

Resource plans will include any of the following, as appropriate:

- table of resource requirements
- graphical summary
- cost tolerance recommendation
- project organisation details, that is roles and to whom they are assigned.

Quality plans

Quality plans include details of quality processes including product reviews, dates of checkpoint meetings and highlight report production. Names of reviewers should be identified, where possible.

Quality plans, developed in accordance with the quality assurance statement in the PID, include any of the following:

- timetable of major review points
- list of review participants and their role in the review
- formal or informal review using a review meeting or only written comments
- any additional information which needs to be taken into account by the review team. Note that quality review criteria should be included on the appropriate product description.

5.17.3 Derivation

The specific inputs depend upon the type of plan being developed. Typically, the inputs include:

- installation standards
- previous plans
- progress reports
- review assessments
- planning experience
- decisions based on Management Risk Assessment.

Chapter 5
Product descriptions
Plan

5.17.4 Quality

Criteria   The quality criteria for plans include:

- is the technical approach sound?
- is the plan feasible in terms of cost and time?
- is the plan up-to-date?
- does the technical plan match the resource plan?
- do both these plans match the quality plan?

Method   Formal quality review of the Project Plan before submission to the Project Board for approval.

Other plans to be reviewed before submission to the appropriate management level for approval.

5.17.5 External dependencies

The external dependencies of plans will largely be specific to the project circumstances and the level of the plan. They may include:

- planning expertise
- ability to identify skill requirements to carry through plan
- availability of information on skills available
- ability to schedule resources against competing commitments
- estimating expertise.

5.18 Product Breakdown Structure (PBS)

5.18.1 Purpose

The Product Breakdown Structure is a hierarchy of the products which must be produced to hold all the required information for a project to run successfully. The products cover management, technical and quality issues.

Each product in the PBS hierarchy should be included for a clearly understood purpose.

5.18.2 Composition

The PBS consists of a structure chart where boxes represent products with composition indicated by lines.

The top box consists of three boxes covering management, technical and quality products. Each of these three boxes consists of several products which are composed of simpler products.

The PBS is supported by a set of product descriptions (see section 5.19) which cover all the identified products in the PBS.

Format and presentation will be in accordance with site standards. An exemplar PBS is shown in Chapter 4.

5.18.3 Derivation

The PBS is derived from:

- project documentation
- installation standards
- exemplar GEMINI PBS.

5.18.4 Quality

The PBS is produced during planning activities.

Criteria

The Product Breakdown Structure quality criteria include:

- does it follow installation standards?
- does it show all the boxes present on the site standard Product Breakdown Structure? Or explain why not?

- have boxes been added which were not on the site standard structure? If so, are the reasons for this included?
- does the structure obey the rule that the totality of the boxes beneath must represent exactly what is represented by the box above?
- does the structure include all products that are to be produced within the project?
- is it clear how each product will be obtained, for example, developed by the project, provided by another named project, already exists, to be bought in from an external supplier?
- is it clear which products shown on the exemplar PBS are not required for this project?
- is the numbering system for the products in the structure in accordance with site standards?
- are all product names unique?
- if a PBS is drawn over several pages, is the relationship between the various pages of the structure clear?
- is there a single box at the top entitled Project Products?

Method	Formal review

5.18.5 External dependencies

The external dependencies of a PBS include:

- availability of a clear project brief
- availability of skills to determine the correct breakdown
- availability of tools to produce diagrams
- project specific dependencies.

5.19 Product description

5.19.1 Purpose

The purpose of a product description is to give a full and accurate description of a product.

This section must hold a specification of the purpose of the product or component described. For clarity, this may be expressed in terms of the objectives for using the product.

5.19.2 Composition

The following description defines the usual components required for a complete description of any product which is to be developed within a project.

Heading information

This provides the unique identification for the product being developed, and includes:

- name
- identifier.

Composition or breakdown

Basic details of the required contents of the product should be defined. The characteristics of the product, other than quality or content should be described, if they are necessary to convey a complete description of the product.

A diagram may be provided to show the structure of a product which is composed of several other products. This diagram is used to show how the individual components fit together to make up the whole product.

A small product can reasonably be described as a report, a form or a document. Standards of layout and presentation may be incorporated or cross-referenced for large products. A description of the technology to be used to create the product may be included.

Derivation	Each product description is derived from: • installation standards for project management • specific GEMINI exemplars, where appropriate.
Quality	This section covers any information on the processes and techniques to develop a product which is relevant to the product description. There are two specific aspects: • *criteria* - against which quality is assessed • *method* - used for assessing the product and signing it off when it is of an acceptable standard. These should encompass the points at which the quality is to be assessed.
External dependencies	There are occasions when information or resources outside the control of the GEMINI project are required for completion of particular tasks and thus products. Details of the possible problems/delays which could affect the project but are outside the direct control of the GEMINI project should be described so that contingency plans can be prepared.
References	This section can provide references to the techniques and/or activities used to develop the product. There may be signposting to techniques and/or activities which use the information from the product.
5.19.3 Derivation	Product descriptions are derived from: • installation standards for project management • this GEMINI exemplar.

5.19.4 Quality

Product descriptions are produced during planning activities.

Criteria

The product description quality criteria include:

For each:

- are all relevant sections complete?
- is the information complete and accurate?
- is this product needed to complete the project successfully?

For the set:

- are all products for the project described?

5.19.5 External dependencies

The external dependencies of a product description are project and product specific.

Chapter 5
Product descriptions
Product Description

5.20 Product Flow Diagram

5.20.1 Purpose

The purpose of a Product Flow Diagram is to show how products are produced by identifying their derivation and the dependencies between them.

5.20.2 Composition

Diagrammatic showing products (in boxes) and their interdependencies (adjoining lines).

See the example high-level Product Flow Diagram shown in Chapter 6.

5.20.3 Derivation

The Product Flow Diagram is derived by analysing the products to be produced by a particular project and their interdependencies. These products and interdependencies are then presented diagrammatically according to installation standards.

5.20.4 Quality

The Product Flow Diagram is produced during planning.

Criteria

The Product Flow Diagram quality criteria include:

- does it follow installation standards?
- does the structure include all products required for the project?
- are all product names accurate, correct and unique?
- are all necessary dependencies shown?

5.20.5 External dependencies

Development of the Product Flow Diagram is dependent on the availability of the skills needed to produce it.

Chapter 5
Product descriptions
Product Flow Diagram

5.21 Progress Report

5.21.1 Purpose

The purpose of a Progress Report is to provide an assessment of the progress made in the current development activities. The reports highlight problem areas and possible solutions as well as indicating the state of completion of development activities or products. They should be completed by the Project Manager at regular intervals so that the Project Controller and the Project Board are kept informed of how well the project is progressing.

5.21.2 Composition

There are several aspects to a Progress Report which the Project Manager needs to supply so that it is possible to assess if the project is running within the defined tolerance levels.

Project achievements
: A comparison of the project's achievements with the plans for this section of work.

Actual versus estimated resource usage
: A comparison of the actual expenditure and resource usage with the planned expenditure and resource usage. This can be used to alert management to possible problems between major review points. Interim reviews will be triggered, if appropriate, to allow management to regain control before grievous slippage is incurred.

Productivity level
: An assessment of the productivity achieved by the project team.

Issues
: Details of issues which have arisen since the last Progress Report was produced, including:

- exception reports
- requests for change.

Error analysis	Analysis of any errors found during the quality reviews to show:

- the number of errors
- how severe they were
- the types of error
- the types of product which gave rise to technical exceptions.

Method/technique comments	Comments on the development methods and any special techniques used in the project, including details of any problems which arose and suggestions for avoiding the problems in future.
Project management comments	Comments on the project management procedures, including details of any problems which arose and suggestions for avoiding the problems in future.
Additional information	Any other material which will be of value to the Project Board, Project Controller and managers in terms of assessing the progress being made by the project team.
5.21.3 Derivation	Progress Reports are derived from:

- records of events which occurred during the course of the appropriate project activities
- current plans
- documentation produced by the Development Team.

GEMINI Technical Reference

5.21.4 Quality
Progress Reports are produced at regular intervals agreed between supply and demand sides.

Criteria
The Progress Report quality criteria include:

- are all the elements present?
- are the issues detailed in a way to identify the extent of the problem?
- is the report associated with the most recent 'project baseline' (as laid down in the Project Initiation Document or a subsequent Circuit Initiation Document)?

5.21.5 External dependencies
There are unlikely to be any external dependencies for the production of Progress Reports.

Chapter 5
Product descriptions
Progress Report

5.22 Project Initiation Document (PID)

5.22.1 Purpose

The purpose of the Project Initiation Document is to bring together the key information needed to start the project on a sound basis and to convey that information to all concerned with the project.

The Project Board must approve the Project Initiation Document (PID) before a project can formally start. The PID is a project management product designed to contain all the information required by a project team at the start of a new project.

The PID contains the project *terms of reference*. The PID contains the definition of the initial *project baseline* by detailing for project management the scope and objectives for the project along with a description of the overall approach to be taken.

5.22.2 Composition

The PID holds differing levels of detail depending on the type of project. For example, the PID for a Feasibility Study will be much less detailed than that for a Full Study.

Each PID is different but needs to include descriptions of the following:

- aims and objectives
- project boundary
- project definition or functional definition
- quality assurance statement
- project organisation.

The project plans cover the technical, resource and quality implications. These are appended to the PID and form an integral part of it.

Chapter 5
Product descriptions
Project Initiation Document (PID)

Aims and objectives — This section provides details of the appropriate business objectives which the planned information system will support once it becomes operational. The information must include a description of the intended benefits, risks and costs of implementing the proposed information system. To provide a justification for the work, this section needs to include:

- *project objectives*, the goals that the project is intended to achieve. Critical requirements of the planned information system should be highlighted

- *business objectives*, the significant attainments that mark progress towards achieving the organisation's aims. The project management needs to be aware of relevant business objectives to ensure that the planned information system is consistent with them

- *business benefits*, the financial and non-financial benefits that are intended to accrue to the organisation through the implementation of the proposed information system. These benefits should be quantified to facilitate an objective assessment of the implemented system.

Project boundary — The project boundary provides a description of relationships with other projects and areas of common interest together with overviews of common outputs and inputs. This boundary includes the definition of possible constraints on the project, such as:

- installation standards recommending IT best practices for the organisation, for example:
    - national or departmental standards
    - installation practices

- existing IT environment. This includes details of hardware, and system and application software, currently used within the business area. Details may cover:
  - communication standards
  - data management
  - communication architecture
  - IT infrastructure
- information architecture. This aspect provides a description of a structure on which the information needs of the business can be implemented to make the best corporate use of information as a resource. Issues may include:
  - data dictionary standards to be used
  - the ownership of the data
  - data administration
  - Electronic Data Interchange
- plans for related products to provide information on issues of:
  - shared data
  - access requirements
  - capacity requirements
  - hardware availability
  - compatibility.

Project definition

The project definition or functional description is an initial outline description of the major deliverables of the project and the activities to develop them. The known requirements of the system are stated as the functional, or necessary operational features, which may be qualified by non-functional requirements.

This section is used to detail the methods and support techniques to be used for the analysis and design tasks.

Quality assurance statement	The quality assurance statement identifies the overall approach to be taken to ensure that the developed products are of an acceptable standard throughout the project.

There are four major aspects to the requirements to achieve prescribed quality. These are:

- identification of quality processes for the project, including references to applicable policies, codes of practice and standards
- determination of overall quality requirements for products and development activities including formats, methods and applicable standards
- identification of the control mechanism to be used in the project to ensure the quality of products and control the use of resources. These control mechanisms include:
  - change control procedures
  - control points of Project Board interest including checkpoint meetings and highlight report production
  - tolerances
  - metrics
  - review procedures
- mechanisms for review and improvement of the quality processes for the project to ensure it fulfils its objectives.

These requirements cover issues such as how the Project Assurance Team will fulfil the role and how product reviews will be undertaken |
| Project organisation | The project organisation structure is defined in terms of roles. Where appropriate, individuals are assigned to these roles. |

5.22.3 Derivation

The PID is derived from installation standards for project management taking account of GEMINI.

5.22.4 Quality

The PID is developed during the initial review of the project.

Criteria

The quality criteria for the PID include:

- are all the components present?
- are names shown against roles, where these can be identified at this stage of the project?
- have the people named agreed to act and to commit the time as scheduled?
- have dates been set for control meetings and report production?
- have the Project Plans been quality reviewed and approved?

Method

Formal review before submission to Project Board for approval.

5.22.5 External dependencies

The external dependencies of a PID include:

- existence of project management procedures
- existence of installation standards.

Chapter 5
Product descriptions
Project Initiation Document (PID)

5.23 Rejected Technical Environment Options

5.23.1 Purpose

The purpose of the Rejected Technical Environment Options product is to provide a record of the options for the implementation of the system which were analysed but not recommended. The product provides an audit of why options were rejected.

5.23.2 Composition

The Rejected Technical Environment Options product is composed in the same format as a Technical Environment Option (section 5.26) with additional text detailing the reasons for rejection of each rejected option.

5.23.3 Derivation

The Rejected Technical Environment Options product is derived from :

- Technical Environment Options
- documentation of the process of selecting the technical environment.

5.23.4 Quality

The Rejected Technical Environment Options product is developed during the Technical Environment Definition activity.

Criteria

The Rejected Technical Environment Option quality criteria include:

For each

- are the rejection reasons valid and adequately described?
- is the option presented as it was presented to the selection process?

For the set

- does the set represent all of the options considered and then rejected.

5.23.5 External dependencies   Any external dependencies will be organisation and project specific.

5.24 Selected Application Model

5.24.1 Purpose

The purpose of a Selected Application Model is to provide the description and scope of the application under development. The Selected Application Model presents a representation of the tasks and dataflows in the application.

The Selected Application Model details the size, nature and complexity of a specific application. This model represents the first detailed look at technical feasibility and establishes costs for the development of an application. An identification of the elements of the application which are suitable for development using knowledge-based system techniques is included within this product.

5.24.2 Composition

The Selected Application Model consists of the:

- description
- scope
- objectives
- constraints
- jobs
- tasks

of an application.

5.24.3 Derivation

- Project Initiation Document
- documentation of existing systems
- interviews with the Domain Team
- Feasibility Report
- Application Requirements Model
- Business Domain Model.

Chapter 5
Product descriptions
Selected Application Model

5.24.4 Quality

The outline Selected Application Model is developed in Feasibility Study and enhanced during System Modelling.

Criteria

The Selected Application Model quality criteria include:

- are the objectives of the application specified clearly?

- are acceptance criteria, for the developed application, identified and measurable?

- are all business constraints covered by corresponding application constraints?

- have all risks to the successful development of the application been identified?

- is the scope of the application clearly specified?

- are any other systems to which the proposed application must interface identified?

- are proposed interfaces to other systems and to personnel identified?

- are the main business functions of the application identified in easily understood non-technical language? Is any specialist terminology explained?

- are proposed knowledge based components identified?

5.24.5 External dependencies

The external dependencies of the Selected Application Model include:

- management availability to provide sufficient information to compile the product

- availability of external reviewers

- organisation and project specific dependencies.

5.25 Technical Environment Description

5.25.1 Purpose

The purpose of a Technical Environment Description is to set out the requirements that must be satisfied by the chosen implementation environment to fully support the operation of the application. There may be aspects which relate to maintenance and general requirements for operations.

Details may be given for a separate technical environment to support the development of the implemented system. In this situation, details of transferring the application from the development to the operational environment must be provided.

5.25.2 Composition

The appropriate hardware environment and software tools for the development and delivery of the application will be selected based on detail defined within this product. The Technical Environment Description will include knowledge base systems tools, but may cover a wide range of other technical details.

The required information includes the following details:

- hardware requirements and constraints
- software requirements and constraints including and imposed by techniques used in analysis and design
- interface requirements for the users and other systems
- system size and performance requirements
- fallback and recovery arrangements
- access rights including access and security methods
- requirements for and constraints associated with hardware and software maintenance

- impact analysis which covers any impact that the system makes on the organisation. The following issues are explicitly explored:
    - take-on
    - testing
    - training
    - user manual production
    - organisational considerations
- system description, which provides a brief summary of the functionality the system is required to provide.

Constraints may also be identified, these may include:

- budget
- identification of the validity of choosing different environments for development and operations.

5.25.3 Derivation

The Technical Environment Description is derived from:

- Installation standards
- procurement procedures
- Functional Design Model.

5.25.4 Quality

Criteria

The Technical Environment Description quality criteria include:

- is the Technical Environment Description technically feasible and viable?
- is the Technical Environment Description consistent with any constraints identified for the project?

- does this product clearly reflect technical policies or documented managerial preferences?
- are the following aspects covered?
  - resource implications
  - service and performance requirements
  - security.

5.25.5 External dependencies

The external dependencies of the Technical Environment Description include:

- knowledge of the capabilities of a range of tools which could possibly be used to implement the application
- availability of capacity planners to evaluate the system sizing information
- requirements of the procurement policy
- organisation and project specific dependencies.

Chapter 5
Product descriptions
Technical Environment Description

5.26 Technical Environment Options

5.26.1 Purpose The purpose of the Technical Environment Options is to describe the reasonable options for the implementation of the system, in sufficient detail to support choice.

5.26.2 Composition The Technical Environment Options consist of a brief system description which is supported by the Functional Design Model (see section 5.10), and for each option presented:

- outline Technical Environment Description
- the ramifications of pursuing this technical environment option. This should include some initial statement concerning training requirements
- Cost-Benefit analysis
- other supporting documentation to support the selection process, which may include an outline capacity planning assessment.

5.26.3 Derivation The Technical Environment Options product is derived from:

- installation standards
- procurement procedures, where appropriate
- Functional Design Model.

Chapter 5
Product descriptions
Technical Environment Options

5.26.4 Quality

The Technical Environment Options product is developed during the Technical Environment Definition activity.

Criteria

The Technical Environment Option quality criteria include:

For each option:

- is the Outline Technical Environment Description technically feasible and viable?
- is the Outline Technical Environment Description consistent with any constraints identified for the project?
- does this product clearly reflect technical policies and documented managerial preferences?
- are the following aspects covered?
    - resource implications
    - service and performance requirements
    - security
    - user interface.

For the set:

- are several viable options recorded with sufficient detail to inform the decision-making process?

5.26.5 External dependencies

The external dependencies of the Technical Environment Options include:

- knowledge of the capabilities of tools which could possibly be used to implement the application
- organisation and project specific dependencies.

5.27 Work structure

5.27.1 Purpose

The purpose of a work structure is to show the project activities in a logical sequence enabling the timescales to be estimated and work to be scheduled so that the relevant products can be developed in an effective, efficient manner.

5.27.2 Composition

Diagrammatic representation showing interactions between activities. Conventions are documented in Chapter 6.

5.27.3 Derivation

Each work structure is derived from:

- installation standards
- the GEMINI exemplar work structures
- Product Flow Diagrams.

5.27.4 Quality

Work structures are developed during planning activities.

Criteria

The work structure quality criteria include:

- are all relevant project activities shown? Do these suitably reflect site standards and the GEMINI exemplar work structure?
- are all activities being used to develop the products identified within the Product Breakdown Structure?
- is the structure drawn to the relevant standards?

5.27.5 External dependencies

The external dependencies of a work structure include:

- availability of appropriate planning skills
- project and activity specific dependencies.

6 Work structures

6.1 Introduction

The work structures in GEMINI identify activities which must be undertaken to develop the eight development models listed in Chapter 3 and described in Chapter 5.

This chapter covers:

- the high-level Product Flow Diagram (PFD), which shows the products to be developed and the dependencies between them
- work structures and their notation
- control points
- activity description formats.

High-level Product Flow Diagram

The high-level PFD shows the major analysis and design products that are likely to be required by a GEMINI-based project. The dependencies between them are also portrayed.

Activity

An *activity* is the process of creation or further development of a product. Each time a product is to be created or enhanced, an activity is defined to effect the transformation. Activities can be broken down into simpler activities. The completion of an activity should progress the project towards its ultimate goal. These activities need to be scheduled in a logical order.

Each activity must be conducted using appropriate techniques for that activity.

Work structures and notation

During planning, the products to be developed must be identified together with the activities which develop or otherwise transform them. The products, activities and their dependencies can be represented diagrammatically. Within GEMINI, such diagrams are *work structures*.

Control points → Management set criteria for completion of activity within each development sector of the spiral model. These criteria are the trigger which enable that particular development process to stop and the review of progress to begin.

Activity descriptions → An *activity description* documents the purpose of the activity and how it is to be undertaken. It details factors which affect the activity start, such as the requirement for a particular product to be used within the activity.

For each project, tailored activity descriptions need to be produced giving the information relevant to that project. The activity information needs to include details of the techniques to be employed and the skills required to undertake the task. This helps management to identify the personnel required to perform the activity and schedule the resources into the plans.

6.2 High-level Product Flow Diagram

The exemplar high-level PFD (Figure 6.1) shows the major products likely to be developed in a KBS development project and some of the dependencies between them.

A high-level PFD needs to be developed for each project as part of the outline planning. The exemplar provides a particular view which needs to be tailored to reflect the specific project requirements. The high-level PFD should be refined into more detailed PFDs as part of detailed project planning, in accordance with PRINCE principles.

The detailed PFDs should be used to develop work structures, as described in section 6.3.

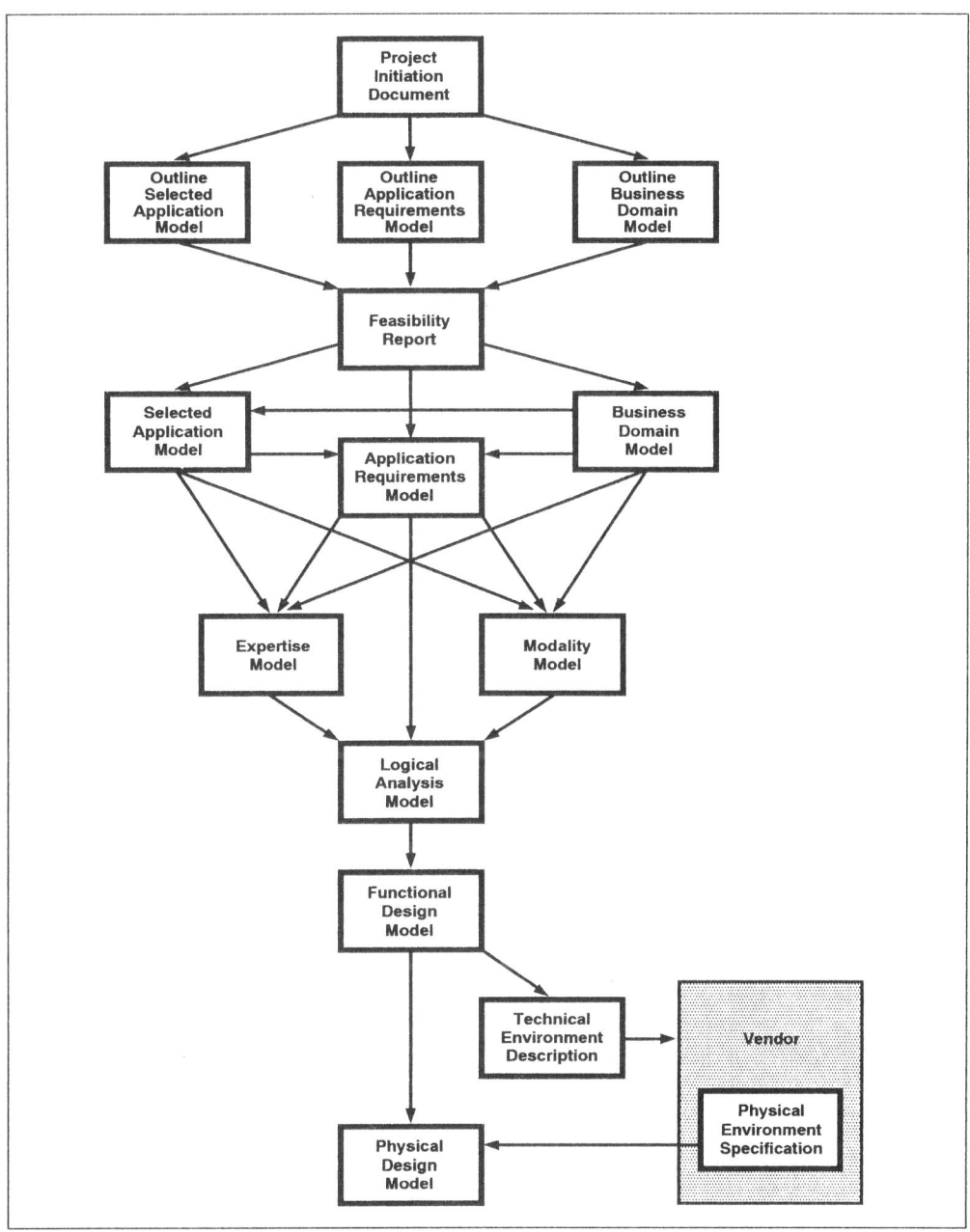

Figure 6.1: GEMINI exemplar high-level PFD

GEMINI Technical Reference

6.3 Work structure

Exemplar work structures have been provided in GEMINI to show a logical progression through a project in terms of the development of technical products. When interpreting these diagrams, it is important to recognise that they illustrate logical dependency but do not prescribe a development sequence.

6.3.1 Diagram notation

It is important to understand the notation used in order to follow the diagrams. GEMINI uses work structures to represent the inter-relationships between activities and the intermediate and project products they generate.

Figure 6.2 illustrates the notation used for a GEMINI work structure.

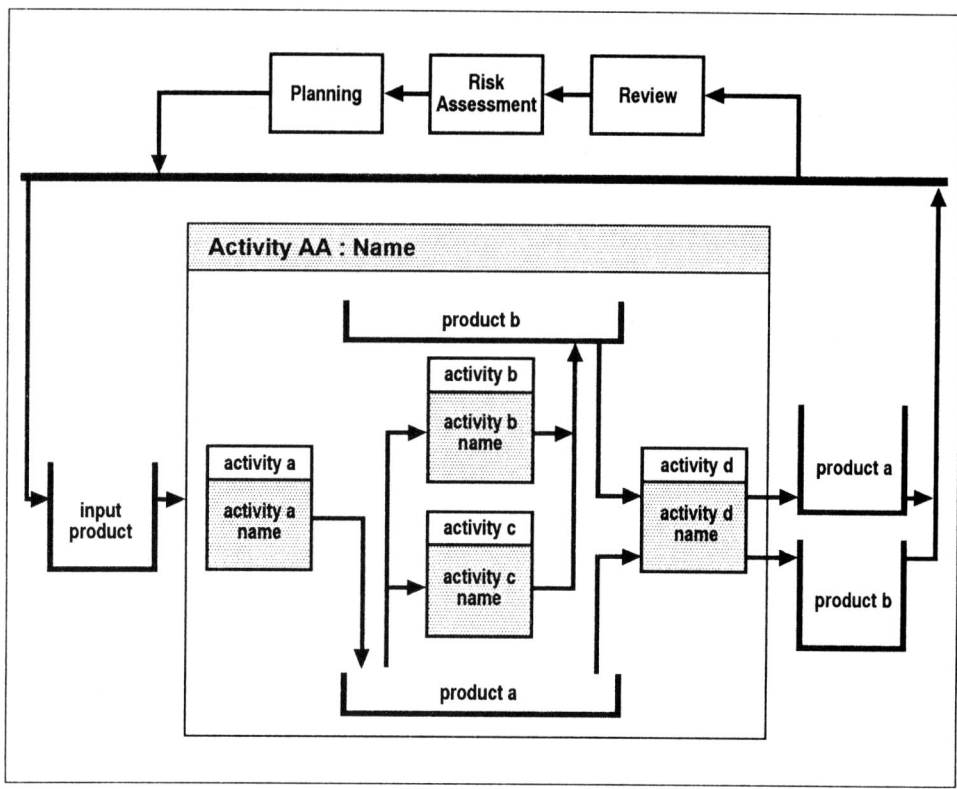

Figure 6.2: GEMINI work structure notation

Chapter 6
Work structures

There are three components of a work structure representing:

- activities
- products
- product/information flows.

Activities

An activity is represented as a rectangle with an associated identifier and the activity name. The inputs needed to perform an activity enter the box representing the activity from the left and the outputs from the activity exit the box to the right.

In the diagram, Activity AA represents a major activity taking place within the development sector of the spiral model. The review, risk assessment and planning sectors are shown above the line, representing the complete set of activities associated with the spiral model.

This illustrates that these are repeating activities where the same tasks take place each time, albeit in respect of a different set of products and development activities. Each of the activities in the development sector may also be the subject of a spiral. The output products from major activities pass into the review sector activities.

Products

An intermediate or project product is illustrated as an open tray with the name of the product.

Flows of products and/or information

Activities generate products and require certain inputs to be provided, either products from other activities or external documents. This flow is represented as a set of arrowed lines between activities and products.

In some cases, a diagram would become incomprehensible if all the product flows were drawn directly. Labels have been introduced to overcome this. Pictorially, these are identifiers enclosed in circles. The identifier in the circle is that of the activity to which the arrowed line would be drawn.

Figure 6.3 shows an example of this labelling.

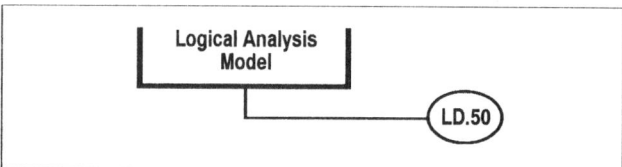

is equivalent to:

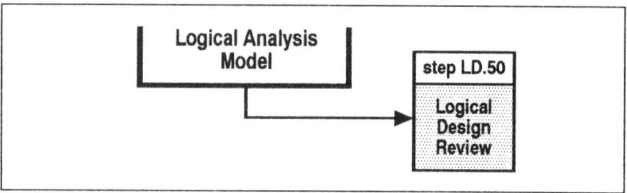

Figure 6.3: Work structure flow notation

6.3.2 GEMINI major activities

All projects need to be broken down into manageable parts. Each of these parts develops products and is a major activity. In conventional projects, major activities are called stages. The end of a stage is used as a stopping point to allow review of the project and detailed planning of the next part. This is an idealised, linear progression through the analysis and design of the system requirements.

In KBS development projects it is rarely possible to complete the development of one application product (see Section 4.8) before starting development of products which depend on the former product. Since the functionality of the system can only be fully defined after knowledge elicitation, it is not possible to separate the processes of analysis, design and implementation in a clean linear sequence. Some revision of the design products and even the analysis products may occur late in the project, as the scope and limitations of the expert's knowledge emerge.

Each application product may be created in one major activity and enhanced in others. Control is exercised at the end of development sectors, but some of the products under development may be incomplete at that time.

Therefore, the ends of development sectors may have to be set according to the passage of time, the use of resources or some degree of development of a product or products (see section 6.4).

The activities to be carried out in a GEMINI project have been grouped into the following major activities:

Activity FS   Feasibility Study

Activity RA   Requirements Analysis

Activity SM   System Modelling

Activity LA   Logical Analysis

Activity LD   Logical Design

Activity TE   Technical Environment Definition

Activity PD   Physical Design

These activities need to be tailored to fit the circumstances of each individual project.

6.3.3 Creation of work structures

In order to create detailed plans, work structures should be constructed for each major activity. The start point for this should be the exemplar work structures, which are described in Chapter 7. These exemplars can be consulted to determine the products required, the activities to produce them and the logical dependencies between the activities.

The work structures help to identify which issues should be addressed during each major activity, and which products should be developed.

Work structures need to be developed to a more detailed level than the exemplars in Chapter 7 in order to complete detailed planning to cover all significant project products.

Additional products may be needed
Sometimes a project may have special requirements or may have to address issues not specifically covered in GEMINI. These requirements and issues may be known at the start of a project or may be revealed by risk assessment and could require the development of products not described in this guidance. If so, suitable products, activities and techniques must be built into the work structures for the project. Constraints imposed by the organisation, the needs of the project or other factors may affect the dependencies.

Product descriptions
Product descriptions document how a product is developed and explain what is required for the final product to be suitable for its purpose. Product descriptions are covered in more detail in Chapter 5.

Techniques
Knowledge based systems development requires novel and sometimes innovative methods and techniques to be used. GEMINI does not direct what methods and techniques should be used.

Chapter 8 details typical techniques which can be applied within GEMINI. It gives an indication of the variety of techniques that can be used rather than providing a definitive list. The techniques have been related to the purpose they serve and, in some cases, to major products.

6.4 Control points

GEMINI has *control points* when the current development work is stopped and review is undertaken. As in a conventional systems development, these points tend to coincide with the completion of a particular major activity.

Chapter 6
Work structures

It should, however, be recognised that the Project Plan often requires that more than one major activity is undertaken at a time. The outputs from an activity may not represent the completion of a product. The most complex interdependencies in a KBS project are between the models which represent the transformation from requirements to implemented system. It is possible to work on models in parallel providing that there are completeness criteria identified, to allow an assessment of the state of completion of a model. Various states of completion of a range of models are illustrated in Figure 6.4.

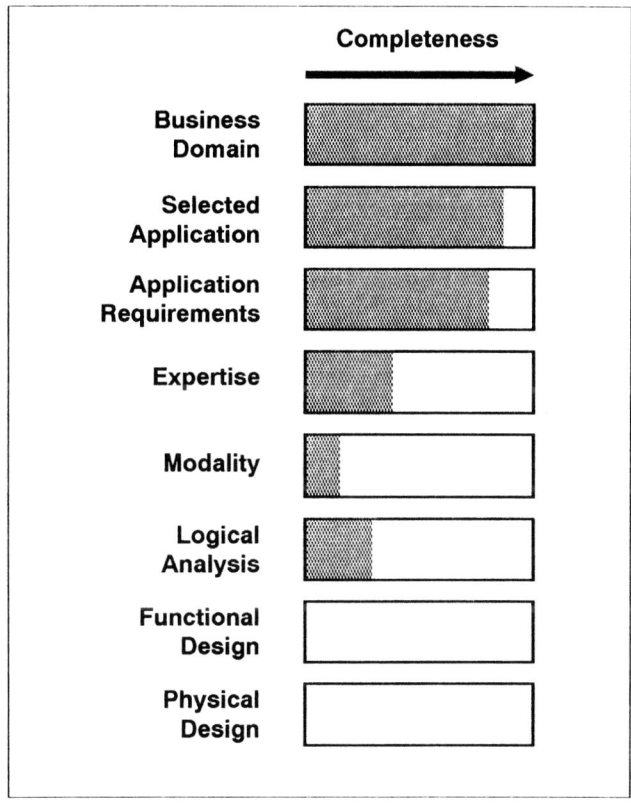

Figure 6.4: Various states of completion of models

The placement of control points needs to be assessed for each project's individual circumstances. In an ideal situation, the following are some of the expected control points:

- project initiation
- completion of Feasibility Study
- completion of the two activities Requirements Analysis and System Modelling
- completion of Logical Analysis
- completion of Logical Design
- completion of Technical Environment Definition
- completion of Physical Design.

These control points should be considered as guidelines. The main constraint is that by the end of Logical Analysis and Logical Design, all the major products except the Physical Design should be complete or virtually complete.

Control at these points is exercised by the Project Board. Similarly, control points will be set within major activities for control to be exercised within the project management hierarchy.

These completeness criteria are documented in the product description produced as part of planning each activity. This documentation enables assessment of progress and quality of product once a control point has been reached. A product must be capable of being used as the foundation for the development of dependent products. All these aspects must be agreed with the users and the Project Controller before development work begins.

The difficulty lies in setting the criteria for completeness of products. It is the Project Manager's responsibility, in consultation with the Project Controller, to define and agree these.

It may be necessary to enforce risk management considerations when defining the precise occurrence of control points. This process may involve stating that work must stop when a particular amount of resource, time, money, or materials has been consumed.

These control points do not conflict with, or override the need to monitor exception conditions which should be tackled using standard project management and control techniques.

6.5 Activity description format

There are several pieces of information which are necessary to provide an adequate definition of an activity. The information must cover the tasks which must be undertaken so that the identified products can be developed.

An *activity description* defines a set of tasks textually, but precisely and formally. It defines and explains the sequence and dependencies of what is to be produced and how it will be produced. The *participants*, that is, those who should undertake the task or the skill levels required are identified. The activities are defined as an hierarchy of other activities and describe the inputs, the outputs, the transformations that take place and the techniques used.

A product description for an activity description is given in section 5.4. Activity descriptions for the GEMINI major activities are given in Chapter 7.

The complete set of activity descriptions, for a project, should provide a level of information which, in association with the product descriptions, is an aid to management for estimating resource requirements and for monitoring progress throughout the project.

Where appropriate, each installation needs to tailor the activity descriptions to suit their existing standards. Each individual project needs its own specific interpretation of the activity descriptions.

6.6 Summary

Any transformation of a product or state of a product is deemed to be an activity within GEMINI.

All activity descriptions should be tailored to the purpose for which they are being used. Thus the descriptions which are included in Chapter 7 follow the general guidance as laid down in the product description given in Chapter 5. The format provides the relevant information for general descriptions. Each project must provide descriptions of each of its activities, tailored to its own specific circumstances.

7 Activity descriptions

7.1 Introduction

The activity descriptions in this chapter should be used as a basis for planning the development of a KBS.

To develop the physical design, which is the basis for development of the operational KBS, it is necessary to establish feasibility and carry out analysis and design.

7.1.1 Activities

The activities described in this chapter are:

FS - Feasibility Study (section 7.2)

RA - Requirements Analysis (section 7.3)

SM - System Modelling (section 7.4)

LA - Logical Analysis (section 7.5)

LD - Logical Design (section 7.6)

TE - Technical Environment Definition (section 7.7)

PD - Physical Design (section 7.8)

7.1.2 Review participants

At the end of each activity, products developed during the activity are reviewed. Each reviewer assesses the product from the particular perspective of their role.

Review participants for the major products are identified in this chapter. The identified roles are the minimum to ensure that an adequate review takes place. The term *client* is used to denote someone who can assess the product from the appropriate demand side managerial, business, technical or user perspective.

7.2 Feasibility Study (FS) activity description

7.2.1 FS objective

The Feasibility Report is generated during this activity.

The Feasibility Study generates an initial assessment of the feasibility of building a system in the area of business which has been identified by a strategy study or project review activities. It takes into account the following considerations:

- business feasibility - potential costs, benefits and associated risks
- technical feasibility - potential technical solutions and associated risks
- organisational feasibility - constraints and impact of the system on the organisation.

It may not be possible to complete the feasibility assessment as thoroughly as would be expected for a conventional system. Within KBS developments feasibility is an ongoing consideration, hence the application of the spiral model.

7.2.2 FS summary

The Feasibility Study activity is shown in figure 7.1. In order to create the Feasibility Report, it is necessary to generate:

- an initial version of the Application Requirements Model outlining the requirements (step FS.10)
- a description of the system under consideration:
  - outline Business Domain Model (step FS.20)
  - outline Selected Application Model (step FS.20)

Chapter 7
Activity descriptions
Feasibility Study (FS)

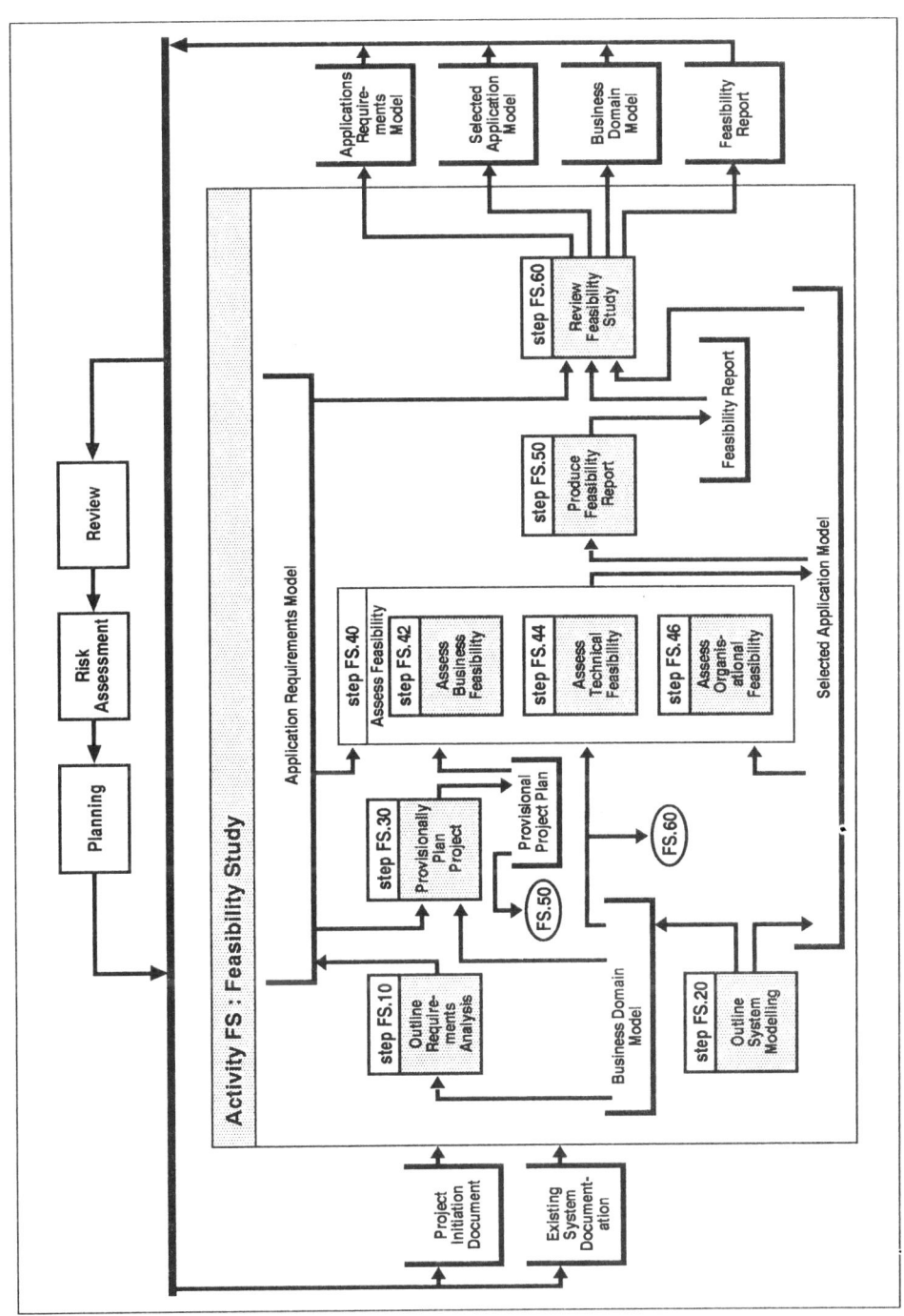

Figure 7.1: Feasibility Study

143

- feasibility options with respect to:
    - Provisional Project Planning (step FS.30)
    - Business Feasibility (step FS.42)
    - Technical Feasibility (step FS.44)
    - Organisational Feasibility (step FS.46)
- Feasibility Report (step FS.50).

When these activities have been completed, a review (FS60) is carried out.

7.2.3 FS preconditions

Management authorisation	Approval of the Project Initiation Document, including plans, by the Project Board.
Inputs	The requirement for the KBS project have been identified at a high level in the IS strategy and subsequently scheduled to support business objectives. Details of the business objectives are documented in the Project Initiation Document.

The inputs to the Feasibility Study are:

- the Project Initiation Document which includes project terms of reference
- existing information about business tasks which have been selected for analysis
- detailed plans for this activity.

7.2.4 FS products

The Feasibility Study generates the Feasibility Report which includes a description of the application, its business environment and a provisional Project Plan. The initial risk assessment which forms a major input to the risk management process is included. This report enables a properly informed decision to be taken on whether to commit resources towards an IT solution to meet a business need.

7.2.5 FS activities

Step FS.10 Outline Requirements Analysis

The Outline Requirements Analysis Step constitutes a first pass development of the Application Requirements Model in order to ascertain the current position of the business, the requirements for improvement from the business point of view and the requirements and constraints that would be imposed on a project by the organisation. The detailed tasks involved include any or all of the steps listed in the Requirements Analysis activity (see section 7.3). The main tasks to be carried out are to identify business system information:

- business need and objectives
- outline user requirements
- outline business requirements
- outline organisational requirements
- outline success criteria for the project.

The main output from this step is a high-level draft of the Application Requirements Model.

Step FS.20 Outline System Modelling

Once the main requirements of the business have been identified, the business system information may be used to construct the outline Business Domain Model. This is used to outline the boundaries of potential applications. Initial construction of the Selected Application Model is begun by considering the nature of each potential application.

Those potential applications which require conventional or manual solutions (non-KBS), are documented for inclusion within the feasibility options. This step involves high-level system modelling (see section 7.4). The detailed tasks include:

- scope high-level system
- construct outline high-level system model
- construct outline high-level data model
- decompose outline high-level system model
- identify potential applications
- outline and determine nature of the applications, that is, KBS/conventional
- construct outline options for the project.

Step FS.30
Provisionally Plan Project

This step is carried out to reflect the requirements identified in steps FS.10 and FS.20. The initial Project Plan is drawn up and links are forged between the business problem, the project approach and design approaches. Tasks include:

- estimating effort required for product development
- producing a provisional schedule.

Step FS.40
Assess Feasibility
(steps 42, 44, 46)

This step encompasses assessing project viability from three perspectives. Each perspective is detailed as a separate step though the steps are interdependent. Options for development are outlined.

Step FS.42
Assess Business Feasibility

The Application Requirements Model and the provisional Project Plan are examined to assess the feasibility of developing the proposed system in terms of business objectives.

Tasks involved include:

- estimating costs - an initial estimate of project costs based on the provisional Project Plan

- problem analysis - the benefits of solving the problem in terms of cost savings and opportunities for the business.

Step FS.44
Assess Technical Feasibility

The Application Requirements Model is used to assess the feasibility of developing and delivering the proposed system using known techniques and tools.

This process may include an assessment of technical skills required and available both within the organisation and externally. Some prototyping of features may be required to help validate potential solutions.

Step FS.46
Assess Organisational Feasibility

The organisational and project requirements held in the Application Requirements Model are assessed in terms of the feasibility of developing, delivering and maintaining the proposed system within the existing user organisation. This assessment includes identification of:

- the likely commitment, within the organisation, to development of the system

- availability of users for analysis of user requirements

- availability of experts for knowledge elicitation

- availability of resources to run the implemented system

- the impact of the system on existing work practices and procedures

- the constraints imposed by the existing IT systems.

Step FS.50
Produce Feasibility Report

In this step, the proposed options are considered and the business, technical and organisational feasibility aspects assessed together. A single recommended approach to the project is documented along with reasons for rejection of the other proposals.

Step FS.60
Review Feasibility

The Feasibility Study should conclude with a review of the following products :

Products under review	*Principal participants*
Initial Application Requirements Model	Expert, User, Client, Development Team
Initial Selected Application Model	Expert, User, Development Team
Initial Business Domain Model	Client, Development Team
Feasibility Report	Project Manager, Development Team, Client
Provisional Project Plan	Project Manager, Client

Subject to a satisfactory risk assessment, a successful technical review of these products should enable the project to proceed to the following activities:

- Requirements Analysis
- System Modelling.

Where an application has been identified as wholly non-KBS, then further work may be taken forward by a conventional approach to analysis and design.

Chapter 7
Activity descriptions
Feasibility Study (FS)

7.3 Requirements Analysis (RA) activity description

7.3.1 RA objective

The Application Requirements Model is developed during this activity. Some aspects of the Business Domain Model are also developed.

It is essential to specify and agree requirements early in the project to establish a sound basis for design and acceptance. It is desirable to bring together all parties concerned with the project as early as possible to obtain their considered inputs and to form good communication links, thereby avoiding problems in later activities. The main steps of this activity (RA.10-RA.50) follow a procedure whereby the requirements are first captured, then subjected to a process of further analysis and refinement.

7.3.2 RA summary

The Requirement Analysis activity is shown in Figure 7.2. To generate the full Application Requirements Model, it is necessary to assess each of the following:

- business requirements (step RA.10)
- user requirements (step RA.20)
- organisational requirements (step RA.30)
- system requirements (step RA.40)
- project requirements (step RA.50).

Having assessed the various requirements, it is necessary to crosscheck them (RA 60) prior to review of the activity (RA 70).

Chapter 7
Activity descriptions
Requirements Analysis (RA)

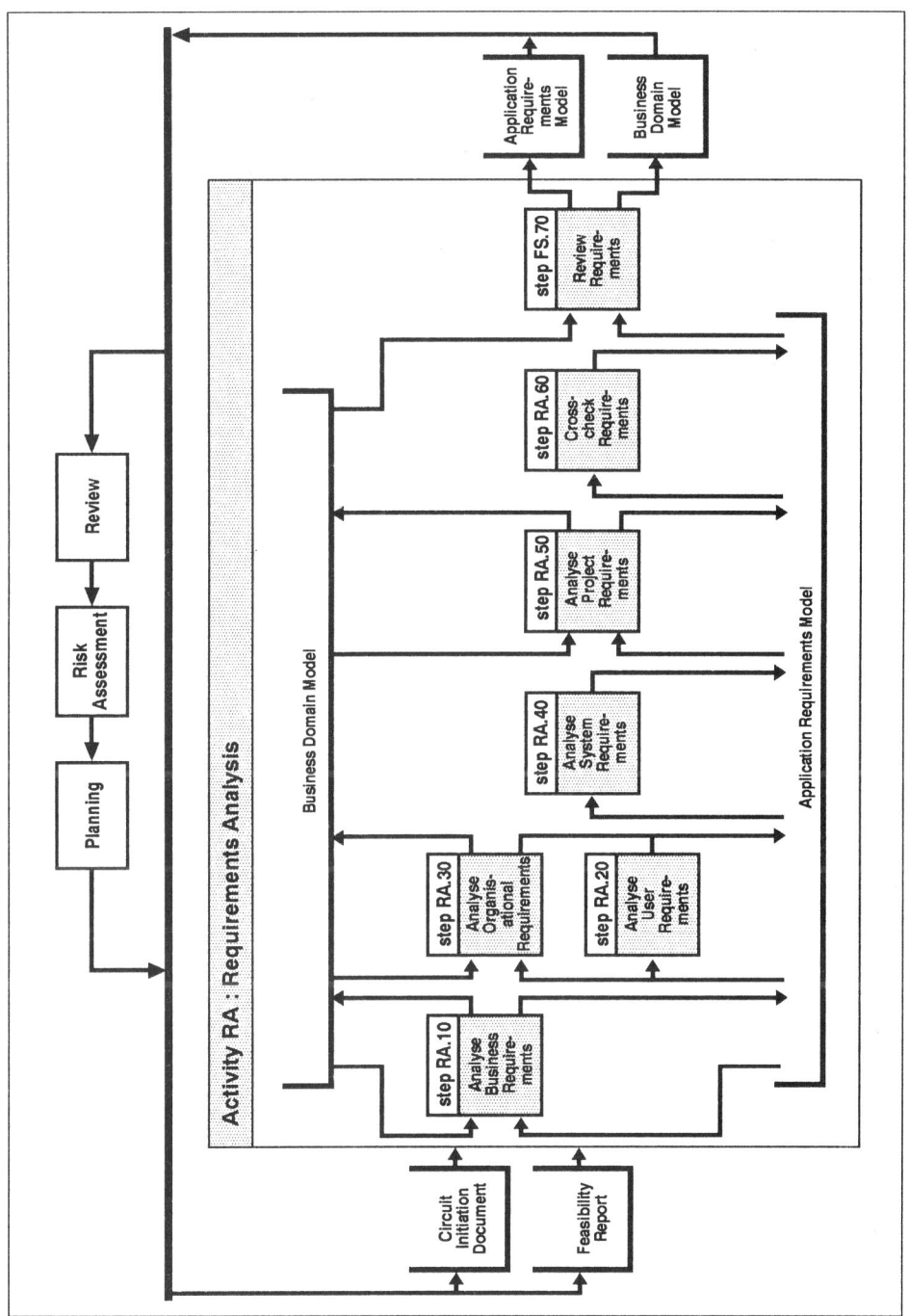

Figure 7.2: Requirements Analysis

151

7.3.3 RA preconditions

Management authorisation	Project Board acceptance of the Feasibility Report and approval to the plans drawn up for this activity.
Inputs	Before commencing the Requirement Analysis activity, the following products are required:

- the Circuit Initiation Document
- detailed plans for this activity
- the Feasibility Report which contains outlines of the business, technical and organisational feasibility.

7.3.4 RA products

The Application Requirements Model is developed by filling out and enhancing the version of the outline requirements as documented in the Feasibility Report. The viewpoints of all concerned with the project must be identified and taken into account during this development. The Application Requirements Model forms the basis of acceptance criteria, and has implications for the management of the project. It is an essential input to the System Modelling and design activities of the system under development.

Some work is done to expand the detail in the Business Domain Model.

7.3.5 RA activities

Each RA activity analyses certain aspects of requirements and relates them to the four environments of the Application Requirements Model:

- operational environment
- development environment
- delivery environment
- project environment.

These are described in more detail in section 5.5.

Step RA.10 Analyse Business Requirements	This step enhances the high-level business requirements which were elicited during the Feasibility Study and updates the Application Requirements Model.

All of these requirements should be stated as precisely as possible to enable success criteria to be drawn up. These are defined as the agreed:

- functionality
- performance
- look and feel.

by which the system will be judged to be successful.

As many of the requirements as possible should be quantified, measurable and designated mandatory or desirable. Desirable requirements should be prioritised according to their desirability. |
| Step RA.20
Analyse User
Requirements | This step enhances the outline user requirements which were elicited during the Feasibility Study and updates the appropriate sections of the Application Requirements Model.

The requirements described include:

- objectives of the system from the users' point of view
- basic functions which the system is to perform
- the level and type of the interaction required between the system and user
- the level of explanation which is required.

All these requirements should be stated as precisely as possible to enable success criteria to be drawn up. |

Step RA.30 Analyse Organisational Requirements	This step enhances the high-level organisational requirements which were elicited during the Feasibility Study. It describes the requirements which must be met by the proposed system for it to fit into existing systems and procedures and the expected impact of the system on the organisation. All of these should be stated as precisely as possible to enable success criteria to be drawn up. Appropriate requirements should be quantified for inclusion in validation and acceptance of the final system. If appropriate, these requirements must be reflected in the Business Domain Model.
Step RA.40 Analyse System Requirements	The requirements defined for the business, organisation and the user are used to produce a set of requirements for the proposed system. These are the requirements against which the final system is evaluated.
Step RA.50 Analyse Project Requirements	The requirements defined in the previous four steps are used to define the requirements for the project. Any additional considerations for the project should also be incorporated at this time. For instance, if there is a need to comply with particular standards for equipment or procurement.
Step RA.60 Crosscheck Requirements	During this step all the requirements identified by previous steps are drawn together and crosschecked for consistency and validity.
Step RA.70 Review Requirements	The Requirements Analysis activity should conclude with a review of the following products :

Products under review	Principal participants
Application Requirements Model	Development Team, Expert, Client, User
Business Domain Model	Development Team, Client

A successful review of these products should enable the project to proceed to the following activities, subject to a satisfactory risk assessment:

- Logical Analysis
- System Modelling. This activity may commence before completion of the Requirements Analysis activity, but may not be completed before the RA products have been formally reviewed and accepted.

7.4 System Modelling (SM) activity description

7.4.1 SM objective
This activity defines the business environment around the proposed application in greater detail so that the application impact on the business can be established accurately. In the course of this analysis, the application must be decomposed at a high level in order to confirm those system components for which a KBS approach is required.

7.4.2 SM summary
The System Modelling activity is shown in Figure 7.3. In order to produce, report and review the Business Domain and Selected Application Models, the following activities are required:

- decompose system (step SM.10)
- model system data (step SM.20)
- identify candidate KBS components (step SM.30)
- assess KBS candidates (step SM.40).

When these activities have been completed, a review (step SM.50) is carried out.

7.4.3 SM preconditions

Management authorisation
Project Board acceptance of the Feasibility Report and the Circuit Initiation Document.

Inputs
The inputs required for the System Modelling activity are:

- the Circuit Initiation Document
- the Feasibility Report
- detailed plans for this activity.

Chapter 7
Activity descriptions
System Modelling (SM)

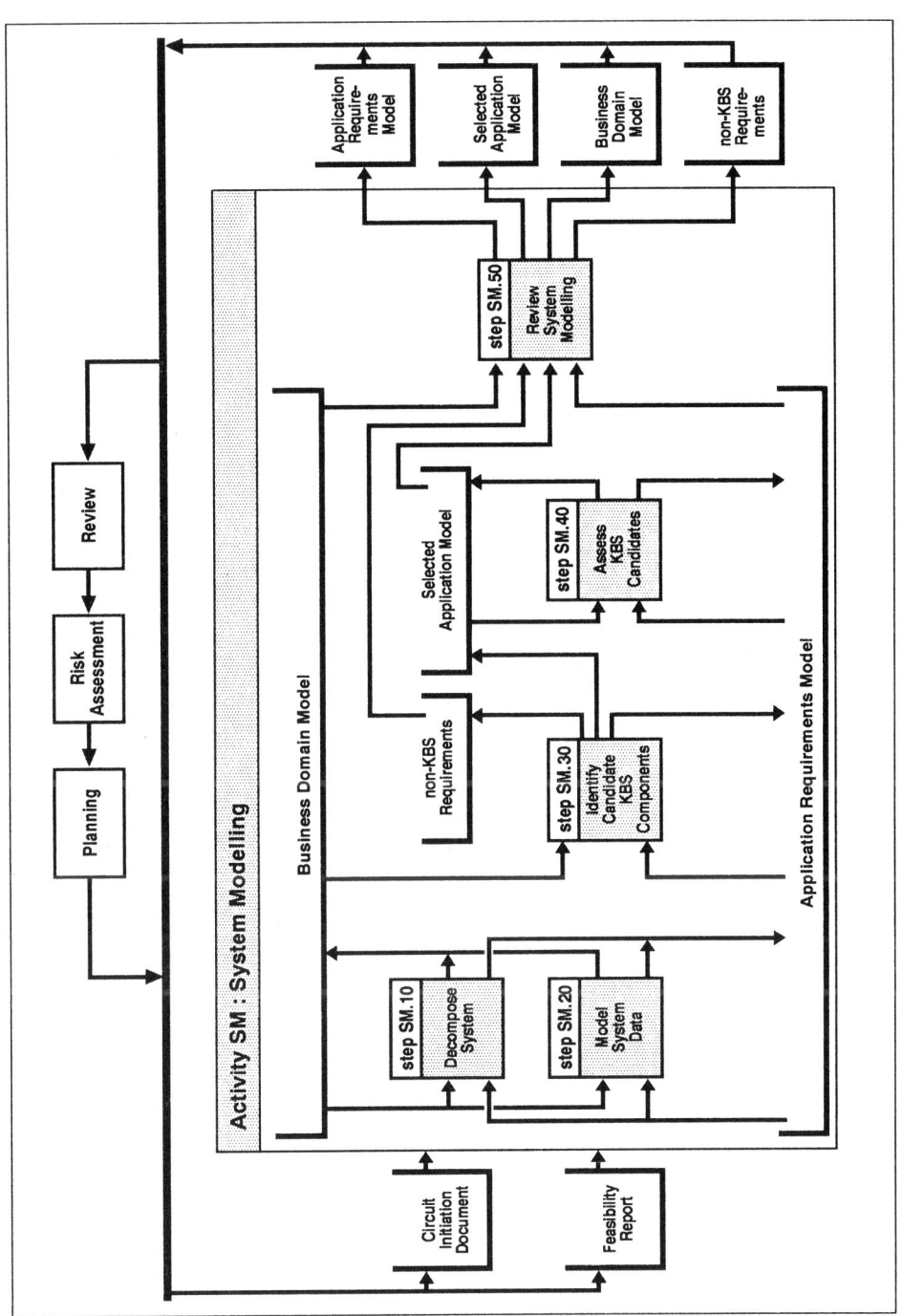

Figure 7.3: *System Modelling*

157

7.4.4 SM products

The System Modelling activity further develops the Business Domain Model, Application Requirements Model, and Selected Application Model.

The Business Domain Model is needed to position the Selected Application Model within the broader business context.

The Selected Application Model is needed to:

- aid project management/organisational management in planning and approving the project
- act as a basis for the work during the Logical Design activity.

7.4.5 SM activities

Step SM.10
Decompose System

The Business Domain Model, generated during the Feasibility Study, is verified and expanded to reflect the requirements analysis. The requirements are mapped to business functions to enable functional components to be identified. Links to systems outside the scope of the project are identified and described. The Application Requirements Model is updated.

Step SM.20
Model System Data

This generates an initial model of the system data for the proposed application which will be common to all system components. This is constructed at the system level and forms part the Business Domain Model. Processing and data used in various parts of the system, or common to other systems, are identified and documented in the Application Requirements Model.

Step SM.30
Identify Candidate
KBS Components

The division of the principal functions into KBS and non-KBS components is reconsidered in the light of the updated Business Domain Model. The aim is to identify those components which have some knowledge based elements. The Application Requirements Model and the Selected Application Model are then updated with the identified KBS components. At this stage, the aim is to identify those elements to be analysed using KBS approaches. This does not mean they will be implemented using KBS technology.

Components which can be clearly identified as non-KBS are not analysed further but input directly to the review step (SM.50). These details can be passed to the Data and Process Design Stages of a conventional IS method such as SSADM. Some degree of iteration may be required between SM.30 and SM.40 before a final decision can be made.

Step SM.40
Assess KBS
Candidates

This step identifies which components described in step SM.30 will be addressed by the system. This entails updating the estimates of feasibility made during the Feasibility Study to reflect subsequent analysis. The functionality of each KBS candidate is described as part of the Selected Application Model. The detailed tasks involved in this step include:

- identify components to be addressed by this project
- determine options
- estimate development effort
- calculate project resource requirements
- determine benefits.

The assessment of the system includes identifying options with reference to the functionality described in the Selected Application Model. It involves definition of the detailed requirements of the application. This allows determination of the areas in which KBS approaches can be used and the extent of that use. Components which are KBS but will not be considered further by this project are also identified.

GEMINI Technical Reference

The KBS components to form part of the project are selected by looking at requirements and the benefits expected against the complexity of development and estimated resource requirement.

Step SM.50
Review System Model

The review of this activity should not start until the RA activity has been successfully signed off.

This review is used to assess the validity of the models produced during this activity:

- the Selected Application Model which outlines the potential options

- the Business Domain Model which represents the current business system and the business system after implementation of the KBS

- the Application Requirements Model which documents project requirements.

Another aspect of the review is to assess those elements of the application which have been put forward as non-KBS or KBS for later consideration. Information on these elements must be suitable to pass on to further studies.

Products under review	Principal participants
Selected Application Model	Client, Expert, User, Development Team, Project manager
Business Domain Model	Client, Project manager
Application Requirements Model	Client, User, Expert Project manager
non-KBS Requirements	Client, Development Team, Project manager

A successful review of these products should enable the project to proceed to the following Logical Analysis activity, subject to a satisfactory risk assessment.

Chapter 7
Activity descriptions
System Modelling (SM)

7.5 Logical Analysis (LA) activity description

7.5.1 LA objective

This activity specifies precisely what is needed to meet the requirements without being constrained by how the requirements are to be met. In order to achieve an implementation-independent description of the system, the Expertise Model and the Modality Model must be created and consolidated in the Logical Analysis Model.

The Expertise Model is produced through the elicitation and analysis of the problem-solving knowledge to be deployed in the system. This knowledge can come from several sources, most notably from one or more Experts and from written material.

The Modality Model records the pattern of interaction between the system and the agent and describes the level of expertise of the users in the domain and the way in which the system will be used.

The Logical Analysis Model is a synthesis of the Expertise and Modality Models and is a result of validating the two models against each other.

7.5.2 LA summary

The Logical Analysis activity is shown in Figure 7.4. In order to generate the Logical Analysis Model, the following activities are required:

- analysis of expertise (step LA.10)
- interaction definition (step LA.20)
- model consolidation (step LA.30)
- validation of the Logical Analysis Model (step LA.40).

When these activities have been completed, a review (step LA.50) is carried out.

Chapter 7
Activity descriptions
Logical Analysis (LA)

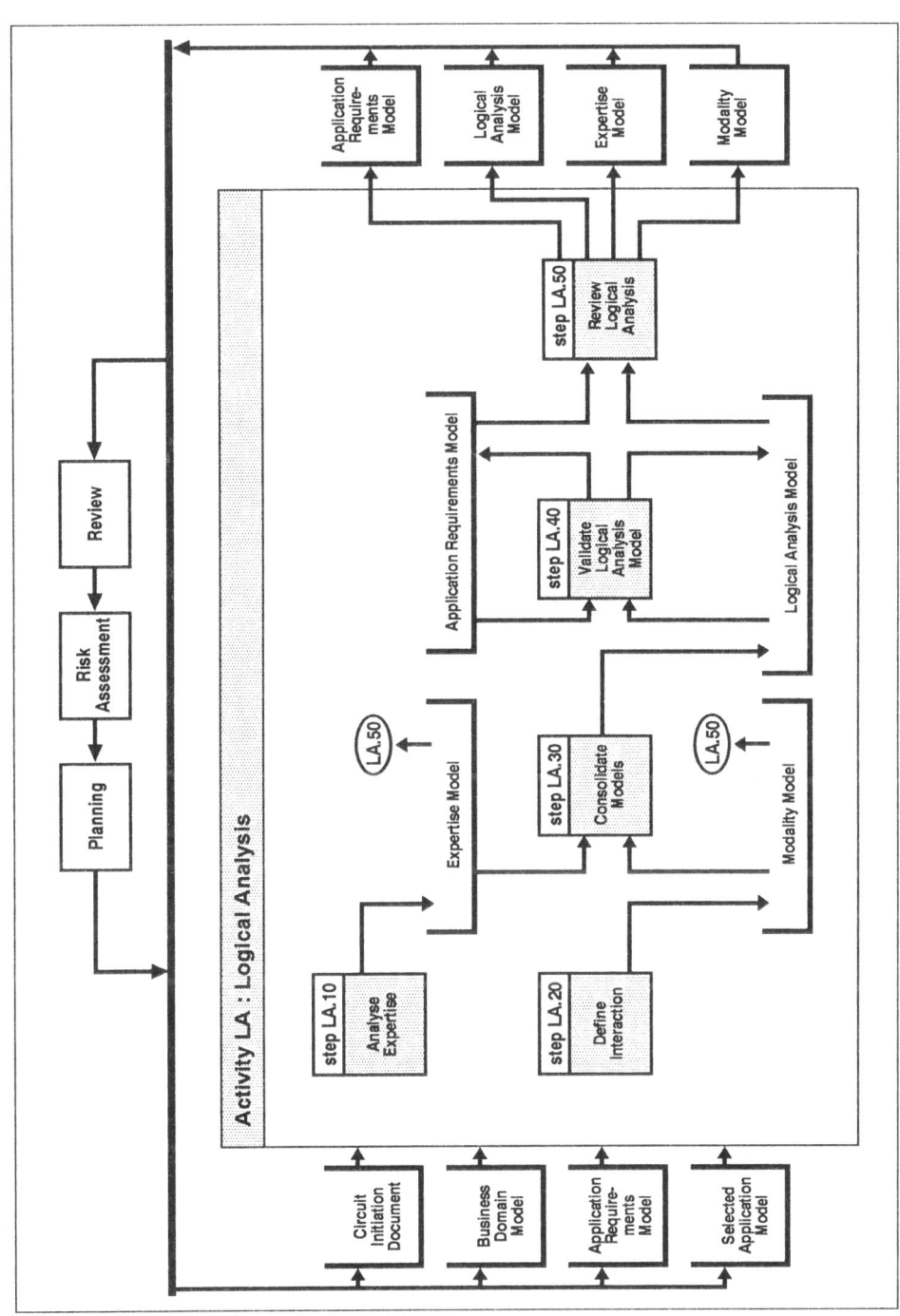

Figure 7.4: Logical Analysis

7.5.3 LA preconditions

Management authorisation	Project Board acceptance of the Requirements Analysis and System Modelling products.
Inputs	The inputs required for the Logical Analysis activity are:

- the Circuit Initiation Document
- detailed plans for this activity
- Application Requirements Model
- Selected Application Model
- Business Domain Model.

7.5.4 LA products

The Logical Analysis activity generates the Modality, Expertise and Logical Analysis Models.

The Expertise Model is a logical representation of the knowledge to be embedded in the KBS component(s) of the system. Therefore, the Business Domain Model, Selected Application Model and expert interview results are needed for its development.

The Modality Model describes the interaction between the agent and system. Therefore, the Application Requirements Model and user interview results are needed for its development.

The Logical Analysis Model is a consolidation of the Modality and Expertise Models.

7.5.5 LA activities

Step LA.10
Analyse Expertise

This step generates the Expertise Model and involves an iteration between the major tasks:

- eliciting/gathering the knowledge from experts or written material
- structuring the knowledge
- validating the structured knowledge.

The GEMINI view of expertise comprises four aspects:

- strategic knowledge
- tactical knowledge
- inference knowledge
- domain data.

See Chapter 5 for more information.

This step may involve the construction of a prototype to assist in the validation of the knowledge.

Step LA.20
Define Interaction

The requirements of the agents are analysed and used to generate the Modality Model. This may involve any of the following tasks:

- describing the nature of the system, such as supporting versus doing
- describing the nature of the agents of the system. This is not necessarily a human operator but may be another piece of software
- defining the nature of the interaction between agents and the system.

If the agent is a human user, other tasks may include:

- describing the level of user expertise expected in the domain
- defining level of explanations, on-line help text
- designing the screens and menus.

This step may involve construction of a prototype to assist in the development and validation of the Modality Model and to gain user acceptance of the approach being advocated.

Step LA.30
Consolidate Models

The objective of consolidation is to bring together the Expertise and Modality Models and to ensure that they are complete and consistent. This is achieved by combining these two models and producing the Logical Analysis Model. The Modality and Expertise Models are likely to be developed iteratively and in parallel. There should be close communication between the developers of each of these models to facilitate consistency checking during development. Consolidation involves a formal cross checking of the corresponding elements in the two views.

Step LA.40
Validate Logical
Analysis Model

This step includes work in three main areas:

- functional checks
- non-functional checks
- components checks.

The results of any of these checks may need to be reflected in the Application Requirements Model, as they may have implications for the choice of implementation vehicle.

Functional checks ensure that:

- the design of the system, as represented by the Logical Analysis Model complies with the conceptual model held by the Expert and User, i.e. the right system is being built
- there is internal consistency between the inference processes and data views of the knowledge.

Non-functional checks ensure that :

- the system *look and feel* will be consistent with user requirements and with the knowledge to be held
- performance requirements are achievable.

Components should be checked to ensure that the system will be cohesive and meet the business need.

Step LA.50
Review Logical
Analysis

The following products should be reviewed:

Products under review	Principal participants
Expertise Model	Expert, Development Team
Modality Model	User, Expert, Development Team
Logical Analysis Model	Client, User, Expert, Development Team, Project manager
Application Requirements Model	User, Expert, Client, Development Team, Project manager

A successful review of these products should enable the project to proceed to the Logical Design activity, subject to a satisfactory risk assessment.

7.6 Logical Design (LD) activity description

7.6.1 LD objective

The Functional Design Model is generated during this activity.

The Functional Design Model provides a complete logical design of the application based on the Logical Analysis Model and specific design considerations.

The knowledge-based aspects of the system have been specified in the Logical Analysis Model and it is necessary to complete and check all aspects of the design before implementation issues can be considered in Physical Design.

Additional information is needed to complete the design of the application including details of the interaction of the system with the rest of the world; for example, by means of data storage and system interfaces.

7.6.2 LD summary

The Logical Design activity is shown in Figure 7.5. In addition to the generation of the Functional Design Model, it is necessary to generate the Outline Test Plan for the system.

The activities required within Logical Design are:

- analysis of external system interfaces (step LD.10)
- functional design (step LD.20)
- outline test planning (step LD.30)
- refine estimates of sizing and implementation effort (step LD.40).

When these activities have been completed, a review (step LD.50) is carried out.

Chapter 7
Activity descriptions
Logical Design (LD)

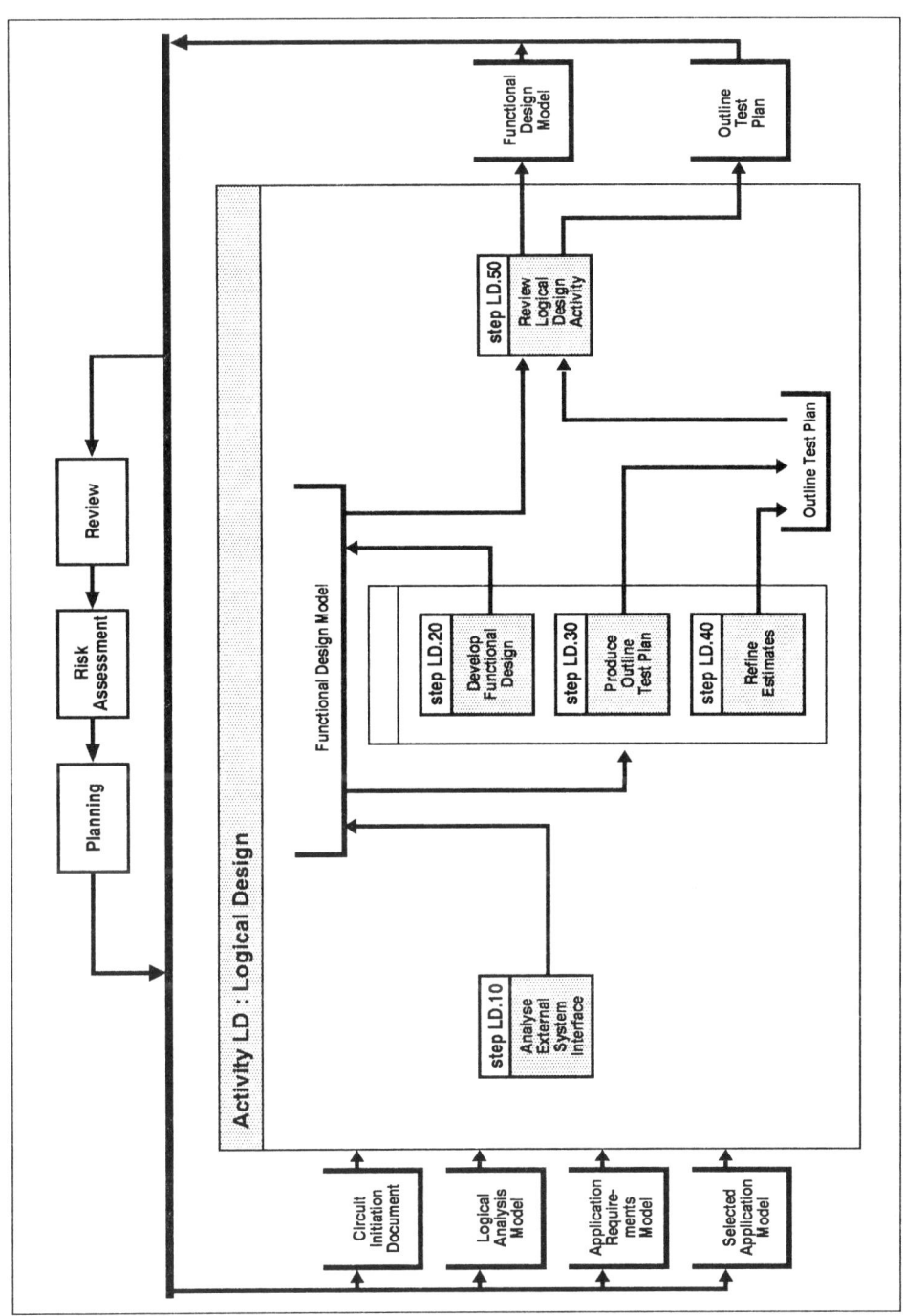

Figure 7.5: Logical Design

7.6.3 LD Preconditions

Management authorisation	Project Board approval of the Logical Analysis Model and the Circuit Initiation Document.
Inputs	Before commencement of Logical Design activity, the following inputs are required:

- the Circuit Initiation Document
- detailed plans for this activity
- Application Requirements Model
- Logical Analysis Model
- Selected Application Model.

References	It may prove necessary to reference the Feasibility Report.

7.6.4 LD products

The Logical Design activity generates the Functional Design Model.

Prototyping of the requirements can be used to validate them.

7.6.5 LD activities

Step LD.10 Analyse External System Interfaces

The Logical Analysis Model, constructed in the previous activity, represents only the expert and user aspects of the system. This step defines the additional functions which are required in order to allow the Logical Analysis Model to function in the real world. For example, it adds information on data input, data output, data storage, all of which are external to the Logical Analysis Model.

Step LD.20
Develop Functional
Design Model

The most appropriate knowledge representation forms and inference mechanisms are selected. The Functional Design Model is developed by revising the Logical Design Model using the information produced by LD.10. The revision reflects design decisions concerning the way in which components of the system will be implemented.

The behaviour required of each of the functions within the Functional Design Model is considered in terms of the knowledge representation, inference, human computer interaction (HCI), system interfaces and performance.

If there are constraints imposed on the selection of development tools, these may be allowed to influence the chosen representation.

Consideration must be given to describing the way in which each of the functions of the system will be implemented in terms of the knowledge representation and inference mechanisms. This process may involve some degree of knowledge refinement, as areas of inconsistency and incompleteness are likely to appear as the model is constructed.

KBS components are checked to re-evaluate the choice of KBS components from the knowledge analysis activity. This is to ensure the continuing feasibility of the project.

Step LD.30
Produce Outline
Test Plan

This step should set out an outline plan for the testing of the system. The structure of the plan depends on the nature of the system and the intended user base, as well as project specific requirements.

The Outline Test Plan holds a definition of:

- approach to be adopted for testing
- effort to be expended in testing different elements of the system
- acceptable error rates
- the level of involvement and roles of user and expert
- acceptance procedures, what they are and who is to be involved.

Step LD.40
Refine estimates

At this step there should be a refinement of the estimates from the Feasibility Study of:

- sizing, that is, re-evaluation of the system size estimate in the light of the knowledge analysis activity

- reappraisal of the effort required for implementation of each element of the design.

Step LD.50
Review Logical Design Activity

This is the most important review because of the importance of the products from this activity.

Products under review	*Principal participants*
Functional Design Model	Development Team, User, Expert
Outline Test Plan	Project manager, Client

A successful review of these products should enable the project to proceed to the Technical Environment Definition activity, subject to a satisfactory risk assessment.

Chapter 7
Activity descriptions
Logical Design (LD)

7.7 Technical Environment Definition (TE) activity description

7.7.1 TE objective

This activity generates a detailed assessment of the technical environment for implementation of the application. There may be a need to define the technical environment for developing the application. The information produced must be sufficiently detailed to enable the selection of the technical environment for implementation and development where appropriate.

7.7.2 TE summary

The Technical Environment Definition activity is shown in Figure 7.6. To provide sufficient information for selection of the technical environment, the following activities are required:

- consolidate the requirements (step TE.10)
- define a range of options for the technical environment (step TE.20)
- propose a single technical environment option (step TE.30).

When these activities have been completed, a review (step TE.40) is carried out.

7.7.3 TE preconditions

Management authorisation

Project Board acceptance that the Logical Design activity has successfully completed. Approval of the suitability of the products from the plans drawn up for this activity as documented in the Circuit Initiation Document.

Chapter 7
Activity descriptions
Technical Environment Definition (TE)

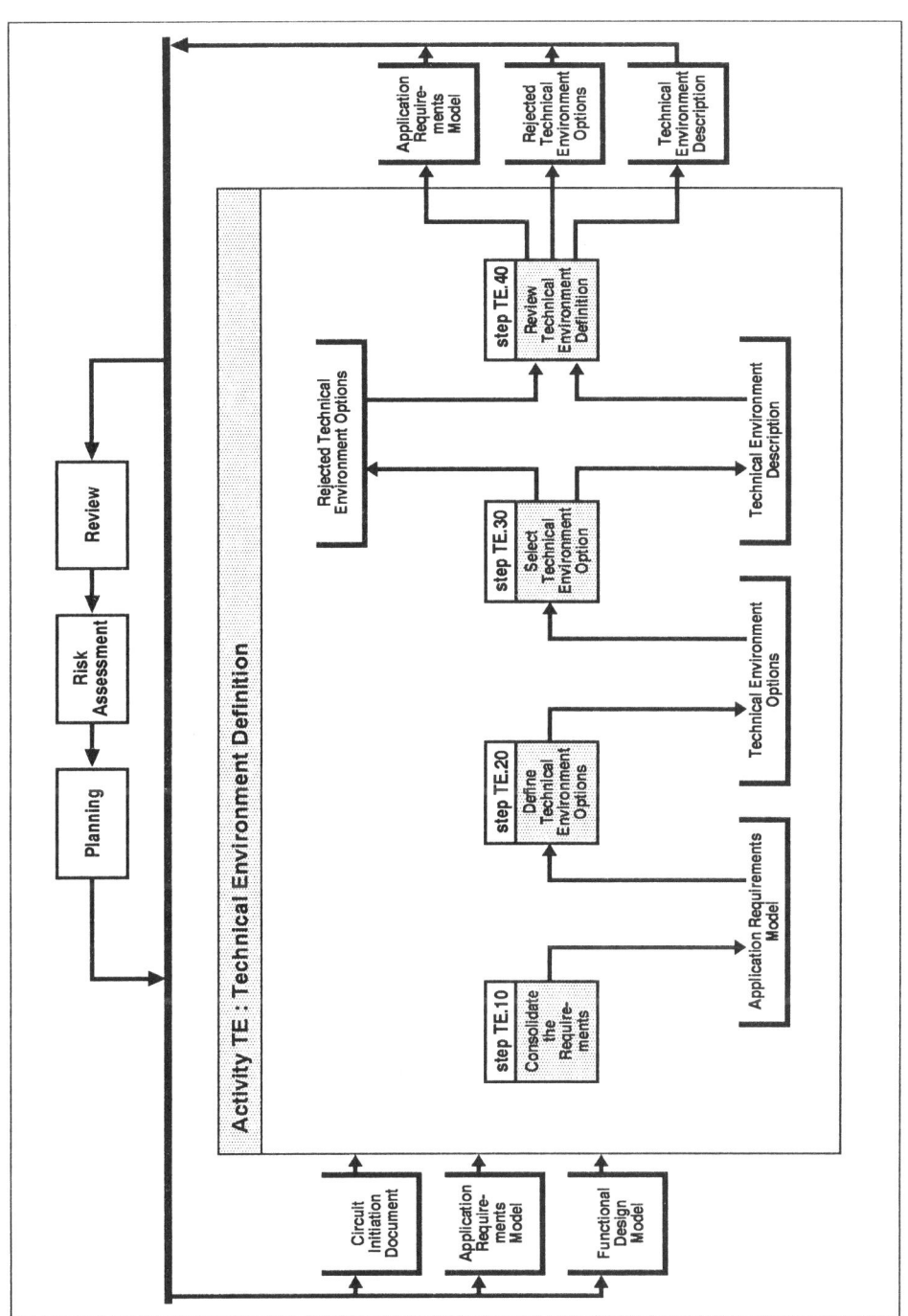

Figure 7.6: *Technical Environment Definition*

GEMINI Technical Reference

Inputs
: The inputs needed to carry out the Technical Environment Definition are:

- the Circuit Initiation Document
- detailed plans for this activity
- Functional Design Model
- Application Requirements Model.

References
: It may prove necessary to reference the following:

- Business Domain Model
- Logical Analysis Model
- Selected Application Model
- Feasibility Report.

7.7.4 TE products

Technical Environment Description for the chosen option and a set of Rejected Technical Environment Options.

7.7.5 TE activities

Step TE.10 Consolidate requirements

Analyse the requirements which have a bearing on the choice of technical environment. Ensure these requirements are fully defined and can provide a suitable basis for acceptance criteria. Identify which requirements are in conflict, such as performance versus costs.

The requirements should be analysed from the following aspects:

- functionality
- type and structure of information to be encoded
- HCI
- interfaces with other systems
- performance.

Much of this analysis has direct links to techniques for capacity planning.

These requirements should be documented within the Application Requirements Model.

Step TE.20
Define Technical Environment Options

Ideally, three or four options for the technical environment should be identified and described. These options should give an overview of how the system will be implemented and the pros and cons of each approach.

It may be desirable to do some prototyping to assess the feasibility of taking some or all of these options.

Step TE.30
Select Technical Environment Option

Analyse the range of options outlined and identify a single option, which may be a combination of several of the proposed options. This option should be expanded and proposed to management as the optimal way forward.

Each rejected option should have reasons for rejection recorded.

Step TE.40
Review Technical Environment Definition

The following products should be reviewed:

Products under review	Principal participants
Technical Environment Description	Project Manager, Client Development Team
Application Requirements Model	Project Manager, Project Controller
Rejected TE Options	Client, Project Manager, Development Team

A successful review of these products should enable the Technical Environment Description to be accepted by management as the basis for progressing the project.

The Physical Design activity can begin when the technical environment for implementation and development, if different, has been chosen.

7.8 Physical Design (PD) activity description

7.8.1 PD objective

This activity generates the Physical Design Model.

In the Physical Design activity, the Logical Analysis Model and the Functional Design Model are used to develop the Physical Design Model and make it compatible with the chosen environment. The Physical Design Model is produced in sufficient detail to enable development of the operational system.

The final design of the HCI and the external systems interfaces are re-assessed to reflect the chosen implementation environment. A revised estimate for building the system can be derived on completion of these steps.

7.8.2 PD summary

The Physical Design activity is shown in Figure 7.7. To generate the Physical Design Model, it is necessary to generate the following:

- data input and output requirements
- data storage requirements.

The activities required in Physical Design are:

- finalisation of behavioural aspects of the system (step PD.10)
- detailed physical design (step PD.20).

When these activities have been completed, a review (step PD.30) is carried out.

Chapter 7
Activity descriptions
Physical Design (PD)

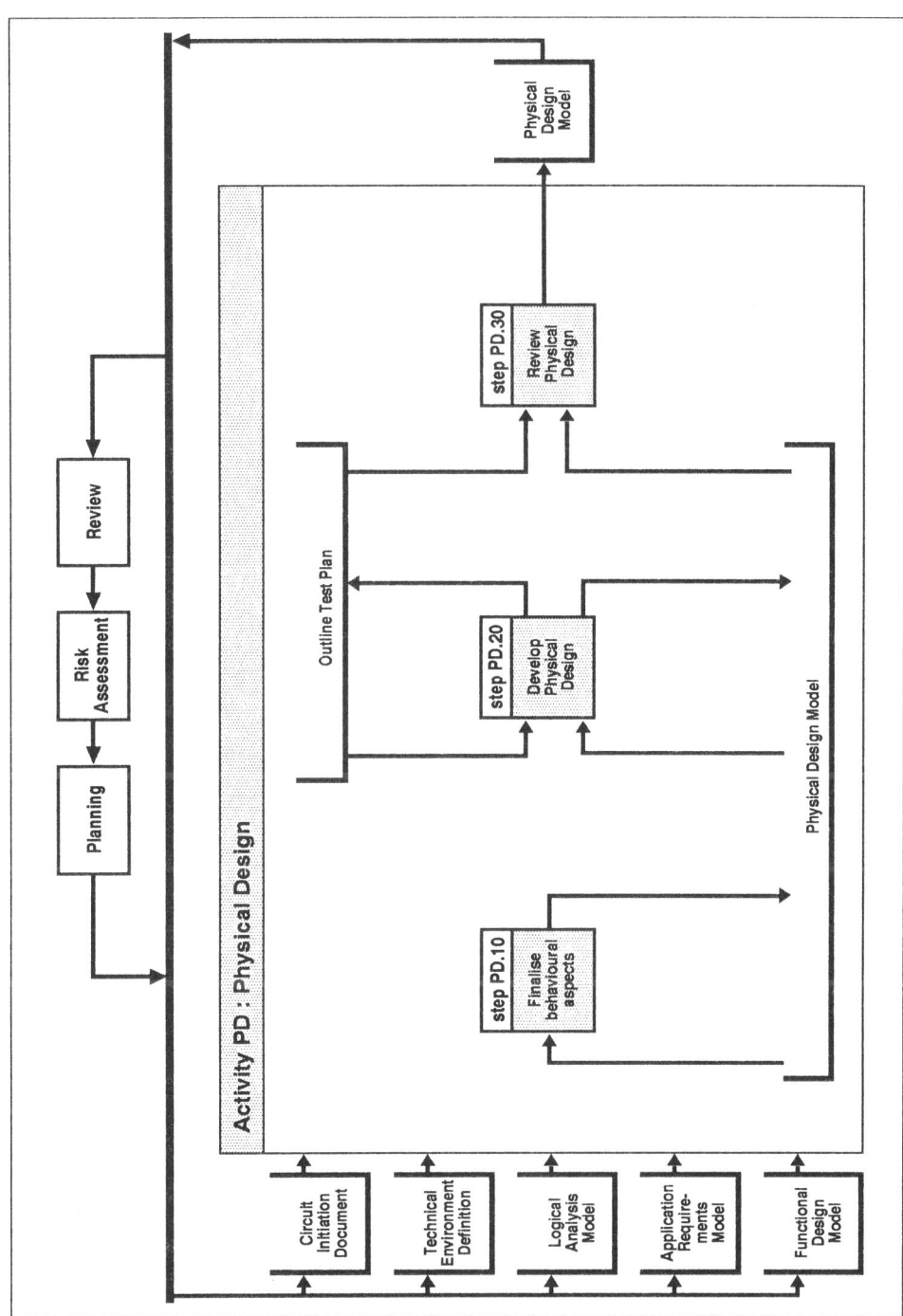

Figure 7.7: Physical Design

GEMINI Technical Reference

7.8.3 PD preconditions

Management authorisation
: Project Board acceptance of the plan and the Circuit Initiation Document and selection of the implementation hardware and software environment.

Inputs
: The inputs needed to carry out the Physical Design activity are:

- the Circuit Initiation Document
- detailed plans for this activity
- Logical Analysis Model
- Application Requirements Model
- Functional Design Model
- Technical Environment Definition.

7.8.4 PD products

The Physical Design activity generates the Physical Design Model.

7.8.5 PD activities

Step PD.10 Finalise Behavioural Aspects
: The behavioural aspects of the application are viewed in the light of the characteristics of the selected technical environment. The required look, feel and performance are matched to the features of the implementation vehicle.

This step defines the precise nature of the interfaces to external systems, which includes details of common data structures, access paths and parameter passing requirements.

The HCI, as defined in the Logical Analysis Model, is used to produce the detailed design of the screen layouts, menus, forms and dialogues.

Step PD.20 Develop Physical Design Model	The Physical Design Model is built by enhancing the Functional Design Model with information about the selected technical environment. This information enables the design to take account of precise implementation mechanisms. The Logical Analysis and Functional Design Models are converted into the knowledge base element of the Physical Design Model, taking into account the structures and formats available in the selected technical environment. This conversion process includes tasks such as: • defining automatic data input and output • defining data storage • defining interfaces to other systems. The high-level testing plan started during the Logical Design activity is refined to reflect the Physical Design Model. Detailed installation planning is carried out to reflect the organisational requirements held in the Application Requirements Model.
Step PD.30 Review Physical Design	It is not possible to carry out a complete review of the physical design without information generated outside the scope of GEMINI. The Physical Environment Specification is required to ensure that the Physical Design Model is compatible with it. *Products under review* *Principal participants* Physical Design Model User, Development Team, Expert, Client Outline Test Plans Project manager, Client A successful review of these products should enable the Physical Design to be accepted ready for development of an implementable system.

8 Techniques

8.1 Introduction

This chapter identifies the main techniques that may be deployed on a GEMINI-based project. The techniques cover the full range of requirements capture, analysis and design. Many of the techniques, especially those used in earlier phases of KBS projects, are generally applicable and familiar to developers of conventional IT systems.

KBS specific techniques form the focus of this chapter. Guidance is provided, covering what these techniques are and where they can be used.

The techniques discussed in this chapter are not a definitive set from which all KBS projects must draw. Guidance is given on the nature and application of some widely used techniques, which are generally available and not proprietary. Many applicable techniques, in current use or under development, are not included.

Choosing techniques

KBS projects typically use a greater diversity of techniques and tools than conventional systems projects. GEMINI supports this diversity by providing a framework into which practitioners can fit the techniques and skills they already employ. The selection of techniques for one model can suggest or constrain the most appropriate techniques for other models. It is important, therefore, that the selection of techniques is explicitly considered and that decisions are reviewed critically throughout the project.

Appropriate forms of knowledge representation will have been considered by the Knowledge Engineers. Decisions on which competing techniques to select must be made explicitly and approved.

Once the techniques have been selected, their use must be mapped onto the product development activities (see Chapter 6). Any one technique can contribute to the production of a number of models and other products.

Range of KBS specific techniques covered	There are no definitive rules on the KBS techniques to be considered in any particular circumstances.

Some organisations encourage KBS project teams to use competing techniques between projects or even on the same project, typically as a risk-reduction strategy. These organisations need to understand a range of techniques which can fit within their development framework.

Some KBS project teams are accustomed to working with a restricted set of techniques and tools which the organisation has standardised. This can reduce costs and improve the maintainability of applications by limiting the skill requirements. Organisations may still have to consider techniques outside this range when:

- application requirements demand solutions that go beyond the scope of their current standards
- new techniques become available which potentially fit within the standards.

The range of techniques that are approved by the organisation may be limited because many techniques are not widely used. This limitation may be due to their specialised nature, labour intensiveness, computational intensiveness or lack of support by appropriate tools.

In order to strike a balance between usefulness and completeness, only widely-adopted techniques are discussed in this chapter. Less widely used techniques are identified in Annex B. |
| Structure of chapter | To avoid confusion, techniques are first described individually (sections 8.2 to 8.5), then referenced to the main development models (section 8.6) to show how they fit in the GEMINI framework.

Techniques are split into two categories:

- KBS specific techniques (sections 8.2 to 8.4)
- generally applicable techniques (section 8.5). |

Chapter 8
Techniques

The description of KBS specific techniques is deliberately more detailed to increase awareness of the range available. These techniques are considered in three areas familiar to KBS project teams:

- knowledge acquisition
- knowledge representation
- KBS validation.

The description of generally applicable techniques covers conventional IT development approaches as well as techniques for management activities.

Section 8.6 provides some general guidance on the selection of techniques before discussing key factors in their selection for the main GEMINI development models.

8.2 Knowledge acquisition techniques

Knowledge acquisition is the term commonly applied to the process by which KBS project teams gain an understanding of the expertise in the business area of concern. The number and variety of sources of knowledge required to develop the system must be identified. Knowledge can be acquired in three main ways:

- elicitation from Experts
- extraction from documents
- derivation from data.

These three ways are discussed in sections 8.2.1 to 8.2.3.

8.2.1 Elicitation from experts

Much of conventional system analysis and requirements capture is aimed at well-understood business processes or tasks. KBS project teams face the problem of trying to understand the mental processes by which the experts arrive at decisions. Some experts maintain that they make decisions based on common sense or intuition. Such decisions may be impossible to model systematically. The subjective nature of expertise means that different experts may have different perspectives of the domain and different ways of solving problems.

Even when the expertise is of a type that could be captured systematically, experts may be unable to explain how they reach decisions. A variety of techniques are often used by KBS project teams to overcome this problem, in addition to interviewing. Interviewing, however, remains the most powerful knowledge acquisition technique for most situations. The way in which interviewing and the other techniques can contribute to knowledge acquisition is described below. The sequence should not be taken as prescribing the use of certain techniques for all KBS projects.

Exploratory interviews

Exploratory interviews, carried out using an open-ended style of questioning, are used to gain an initial overview of a domain, application area or task. The main aim is to cover the area concerned at a high level rather than analyse it in depth. The interviewers' findings have to be presented to the expert to ensure correctness and appropriateness.

Structured interviews

Structured interviews address specific issues in a focused way. Careful management of the Expert's time is needed to ensure that the interview covers all the ground it should. A list of questions is prepared to address all the issues within the planned scope of the interview. This list may be given to the Expert prior to the interview to allow the Expert time to assemble information and call in other experts as necessary. A high level of skill is required by the Knowledge Engineer to establish a rapport with the Expert and make effective use of time.

Case Analysis

Case Analysis involves the Knowledge Engineer and Expert walking through previous examples of the problem-solving process. The Expert provides the details of a variety of cases and the decisions made. The Expert is encouraged to describe the rationale for each of the decisions, and possible alternative decisions on the cases are discussed. The consequences of changing various aspects of the cases are explored. Hypothetical cases may also be considered. Case Analysis is sometimes also referred to as *protocol analysis*.

Chapter 8
Techniques

Simulated work

Simulated work is similar to case analysis, but the case load is contrived to exercise the greatest possible number of decision paths. The technique normally begins by considering commonly used areas of expertise before moving on to the less frequently used areas.

Training

Sometimes it is necessary for a Knowledge Engineer to be trained to carry out a task to gain understanding of how a particular job is performed. *Training* can be used to gain familiarity with the terminology of the domain in question and to acquire an understanding of how decisions about tasks are made. Training is especially useful when Experts are unable to impart their knowledge in terms that can be understood by the Knowledge Engineer.

Questionnaires

Questionnaires can overcome the labour intensive constraint of eliciting knowledge face to face with the Expert and permit canvassing of wide opinion. Questionnaires are particularly useful where there is a very definite and structured line of enquiry. A questionnaire is also valuable where there is no identifiable custodian of domain expertise, so that a number of opinions have to be considered.

There are several dangers in using questionnaires:

- respondents may dislike being treated impersonally
- misunderstanding of the questions
- questions constraining responses
- responses of insufficient detail.

The opportunity for a less formal exchange of ideas and up-to-date organisational information is also lost.

187

Card Sorts	*Card Sorts* are used to derive classifications of objects or concepts from the Expert. Concepts are written on separate cards and the Expert groups similar concepts together. This technique is useful in building the Knowledge Engineer's understanding of the relationship between concepts. It is particularly good at establishing whether terms are synonymous, overlapping or distinct.
Repertory Grids	*Repertory Grids* are a way of capturing format knowledge about concepts, such as objects, situations or events, and the characteristics they display (attributes) in a matrix. The Expert gives appropriate attribute values for each concept included in the matrix. Once the knowledge is collated in a matrix or Grid, the Expert and Knowledge Engineer can see the smallest set of attributes that can be used to distinguish between different concepts. This information can be used to define an efficient set of rules for categorising these concepts.
Wizard-of-Oz	The *Wizard-of-Oz*, or *Mock-up Dialogue*, technique involves separating the User and the Expert and arranging for their communication to be carried out via terminals in different rooms. Communication is restricted to pictures and text that can be transmitted between the terminals. The User has to present a problem to the Expert, who has to elicit relevant information and provide a solution. This technique is particularly good for assessing the complexity of areas of knowledge by capturing a real dialogue. It also restricts the mode of communication to a form that could be supported by a system.
Telephone Test	The *Telephone Test* is similar to the Wizard-of-Oz technique in that it seeks to restrict the complexity of the interaction between the User and the Expert. The Knowledge Engineer concentrates on the advice and ideas that can be communicated by the Expert over the telephone in a specified amount of time. The Telephone Test is often employed to assess which areas of domain expertise can be represented in the system.

8.2.2 Extraction from documents

Documentary sources, where they are available and usable, are a particularly cost-effective way of gaining access to expertise. The information is written so that it is readily accessible without reliance on experts' availability.

A number of drawbacks may apply to the extraction of knowledge from documents:

- many procedures are either not documented at all or are documented in insufficient detail to be used directly as a basis for the development models
- documentation may be too complex for efficient analysis
- documents may be out of date
- not all documents are authorised
- written procedures may represent an idealised form of business process. This is interpreted by the staff on the ground who continually define and re-define corporate practice through their actions
- the language in which the document is written may require specialist interpretation; this applies, for example, to legal documents.

Despite these caveats, relevant pre-existing documentary sources can speed the process of expertise modelling.

A number of important documentary sources are discussed below. No attempt has been made to provide a comprehensive list.

| Manuals, handbooks and operating procedures | There are often manuals, handbooks and operating procedures describing the activities and culture of an organisation. There may be various documents, covering topics from operation of particular pieces of machinery through departmental procedures to top-level policy documents. Where physical machinery is described, documents are likely to be more definitive than where a business or organisational process is described. Many operating procedure documents need interpretation to reflect current policies and procedures.

The Development Team must gain understanding of how documents are used in carrying out specific tasks as well as the knowledge represented in them. Any discrepancies between the written guidance and current practice need to be resolved at the appropriate level of management. Careful handling of the politics of this sort of situation is required. |

| Organisational information | Organisational structures, top-level objectives and current performance information can be assimilated from annual reports and other high-level documents in the early stages of the project. Many facets of an individual's conduct are determined by the organisational strategy, so the Knowledge Engineer needs to gain this level of organisational awareness. |

| Textbooks | Textbooks can contain some of the technical information to be represented in the system. Many tasks require an understanding of some technical specialisation by the person performing them. A Knowledge Engineer may have to do considerable background reading to gain enough background to be able to understand the Experts. |

8.2.3 Derivation from data

Most KBS are built from knowledge that is either retained by an organisation's employees or embodied in its written procedures. KBS projects may also draw upon implicit knowledge derived from corporate information, using statistical or other analytical techniques.

Chapter 8
Techniques

Patterns existing in a database, which only become visible after statistical analysis, are a good example of derived knowledge. Experts often find that such newly identified patterns present insights into the operation of their domain.

Some advantages of deriving knowledge from data as opposed to eliciting knowledge from the Expert are that:

- it can reflect the way that decisions are taken across an organisation, rather than just the way that an individual takes decisions
- it can be used where access to the Expert is limited
- it can be used to provide new insights into how a domain operates
- the process of derivation can be automated to some extent, which allows it to be repeated as new data becomes available.

The main disadvantage is that derived knowledge merely establishes patterns in data present in the database and does not represent the conscious decision-making of an Expert. However, many experts find the approach helpful in discovering patterns and in forming their opinions.

Two techniques used in deriving knowledge from data are:

- Rule Induction
- statistical analysis.

Rule Induction	*Rule Induction* is a technique which looks at sample cases likely to be submitted to the implemented KBS and classifies them into groups sharing common characteristics. This classification is done by defining the smallest set of data items or values that can be used to split the data into two sub-groups. Each sub-group is then split using the same process until there is a pre-defined number of categories or further split is impractical.
	The criteria used to determine which sample cases lie in each group are expressed in rules. The complete set of rules classifies the sample cases into their respective groups.
	Rule Induction can identify previously unsuspected patterns in data. It can also be used to identify the minimum amount of data necessary for effective analysis or classification. The rules are normally in a format which can be incorporated into a KBS with little or no modification.
	There are several tools available to carry out Rule Induction. These tools use algorithms to carry out the classification and define the rules, for a given set of sample cases.
Statistical analysis	Statistical analysis techniques are often used in KBS projects to identify trends and patterns in data. Heuristics may then be defined to isolate these patterns and to identify the same patterns in different data. Statistical techniques are used when modelling events in terms of their probability.
Documentation	The results of knowledge acquisition must be documented for further analysis and translation through to an implementable system. Ideally, this documentation should be structured in a manner independent of application and implementation. Research is currently in progress into structuring knowledge without unduly constraining the way it is used in implementation.

Chapter 8
Techniques

8.3 Knowledge representation techniques

Knowledge representation refers to the formalisms that are adopted to record expertise in a structured form. This abstraction of the knowledge forms the basis for its incorporation in KBS. Significantly, the largest proportion of KBS to date have been built using a combination of just three knowledge representation techniques:

- Production Rules
- Frames
- First Order Predicate Logic.

These techniques are described below, together with other established knowledge representation techniques.

Production Rules

Production Rules are the most frequently used form of knowledge representation. Rules are defined comprising a set of conditions and a set of actions or assertions. They have the form:

IF condition(s) THEN action(s)

Whenever the conditions are met, the rule becomes true and new facts or assertions are made or produced, hence the name. This process may cause other rules to become valid and more assertions to be made.

GEMINI Technical Reference

The example below shows a Production Rule representation in the area of car fault diagnosis. The rules reflect part of the simplified fault tree shown in Figure 8.1.

IF	there is an electrical problem
OR	there is a fuel supply problem
OR	there is an ignition problem
THEN	the car will not start

IF	there is a fuel pipe leak
OR	there is no petrol
OR	there is a petrol pump failure
THEN	there is a fuel supply problem

IF	the ignition light comes on
AND	the petrol gauge reads empty
THEN	there is no petrol

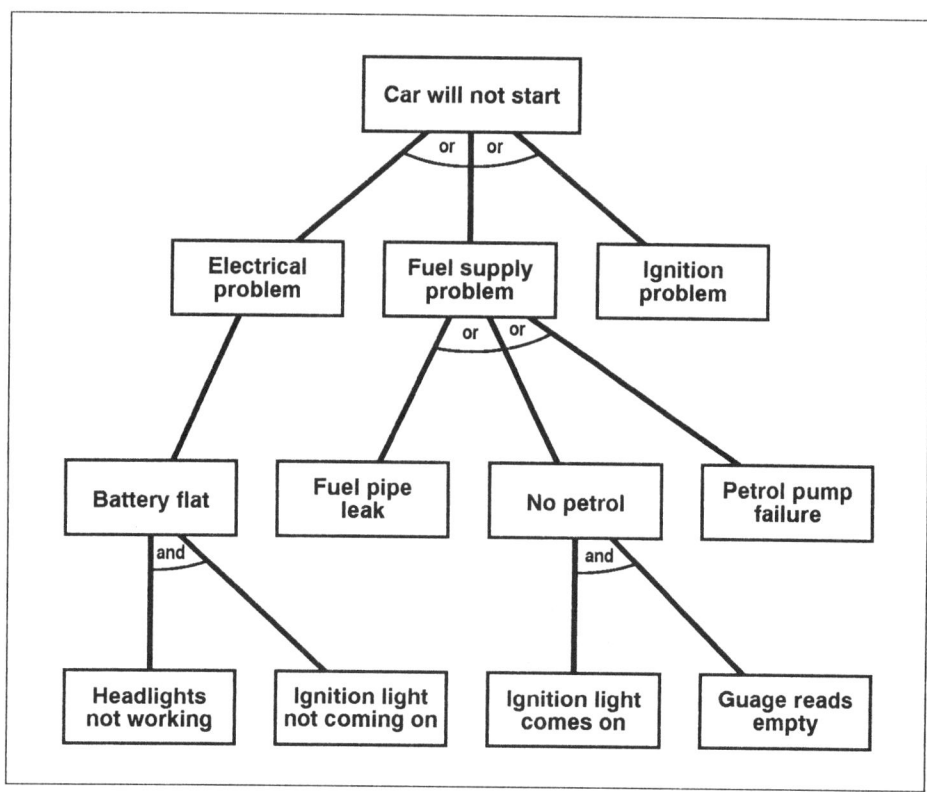

Figure 8.1 Partial fault tree for car fault diagnosis

The process of moving through conditions and assertions is referred to as *chaining*. The process of chaining is also referred to as inference.

Rules can chain from a condition through all the assertions possible (forward chaining) or in the opposite direction (backward chaining). In backward chaining, a goal is established and inference is used to trace back through all the chains of rules establishing sub-goals or conditions that would make the goal true. Backward chaining is often used to represent diagnostic or classification tasks.

Some problems are suited to forward chaining through Production Rules, while other problems are suited to backward chaining. There are options for the order in which Production Rules are used, which may vary from problem to problem. To use Production Rules effectively, decisions have to be taken on how to use them for different tasks.

It is easy to use Production Rules to design inefficient solutions that require many inferences to arrive at any conclusion. This inefficiency arises because a few rules can be made to do extremely complex searches or sequences of evaluation. Care must be taken to control use of the Production Rules. The knowledge base may have to be structured in some way to restrict the scope of inference to particular areas. Forward chaining, in particular, can be computationally intensive.

Frames

Frames are a technique for representing classes of things, situations or events. Sub-frames are defined with greater levels of specificity down to the necessary level of detail. The concept of frames is allied closely to the static data facilities provided in object oriented design and programming. The chief advantage of frames is that they can be used to capture very general descriptions of real-world phenomena, which can then be elaborated as the need for more detail becomes apparent.

The example below illustrates the use of frames within a hierarchy, based on a motor vehicles example. Variables, called *slots* are inherited by low-level frames. Slots in italics have been defined at that level. Values in slots can be inherited from above or provided at the lower level.

Motor Vehicles Frame
  Wheels:
  Engine Capacity:
  Number of Passengers:
  Carrying Capacity:
  Dimensions:
  Number of Axles:

Cars Frame
  Wheels: 4
  Engine Capacity:
  Number of Passengers: 4
  Carrying Capacity:
  Dimensions:
  Number of Axles: 2
  Number of Doors:
  Fuel Economy:

Sports Car Frame
  Wheels: 4
  Engine Capacity:
  Number of Passengers: 2
  Carrying Capacity:
  Dimensions:
  Number of Axles: 2
  Number of Doors: 2
  Fuel Economy: Poor
  Top Speed: 120 mph
  Multi-valve   Yes
  Low Profile Tyres   Yes

First Order Predicate Logic

First Order Predicate Logic (FOPL) is a technique that involves modelling an area of expertise as a set of logic clauses. The technique is also known as Logic Programming. A FOPL representation of part of the car fault tree could look like this:

No petrol :- (if)
    ignition line comes on,
    petrol gauge reads empty.

Fuel supply problem :- (if)
    fuel pipe leak.
Fuel supply problem :- (if)
    no petrol.
Fuel supply problem :- (if)
    petrol pump failure.

Car will not start :- (if)
    electrical problem.
Car will not start :- (if)
    Fuel supply problem.
Car will not start :- (if)
    Ignition problem.

FOPL is frequently used to define requirements in software, before implementation in a different target language. It can be a particularly compact way of representing constraint problems, such as scheduling and routing, since the complexities of the problem solving can be abstracted out of the initial problem definition. In FOPL, the order in which the clauses are written is irrelevant to the processing order. The information must be searched to find which aspects are relevant and affected.

Some Knowledge Engineers regard their logic programs as self-documenting knowledge representations. A problem with regarding FOPL as an adequate knowledge representation on its own is that it is incomprehensible to most experts.

Certainty

Many events and statements about the world are uncertain. There is, therefore, a need for techniques that allow the modelling of certainty and uncertainty. No one formalism exists for adequately representing these, although extensive use has been made in KBS projects of Bayesian statistics and Dempster-Schafer Theory (see Annex B). Varying degrees of rigour have been used in applying statistical models. A common problem is that many of the assumptions of statistical theory concern the independence of variables. These assumptions are not applicable in all situations.

Using certainty factors does fit with many experts' views of the world. These can be used to show that in a given situation one result is more likely than another; or similarly, that for a given result one cause is more likely than another. Certainty factors are sometimes built into the Production Rules formalism. Rules containing certainty factors often have the following type of format:

IF   headlights do not work

THEN (PROBABILITY 0.8)   battery is flat.

Other mechanisms for managing uncertainty are probability and fuzzy logic.

Contexts/Worlds

The *Context/Worlds* technique is also known as *hypothetical reasoning*. It involves taking a real situation and enabling hypotheses to be made about the effects of changes to characteristics of the situation, thus representing what-if type reasoning. It usually takes the form of an extension to the Production Rules approach. In order to compare situations, a set of details is used, then controlled changes made to determine their effect on the outcome.

This technique enables representation of relatively complex operational research situations.

Chapter 8
Techniques

Semantic Nets and Conceptual Graphs

Semantic Nets and Conceptual Graphs are two techniques for representing concepts and logical relations between them. Both are intended to provide a form of knowledge representation that is accessible to the Expert by being highly graphical. Both techniques have suffered from a shortage of support tools. Without these tools, the techniques can require prohibitive amounts of effort in re-drawing the diagrams to keep up with changes in understanding.

Figure 8.2 shows a semantic net of a simplified view on road accidents.

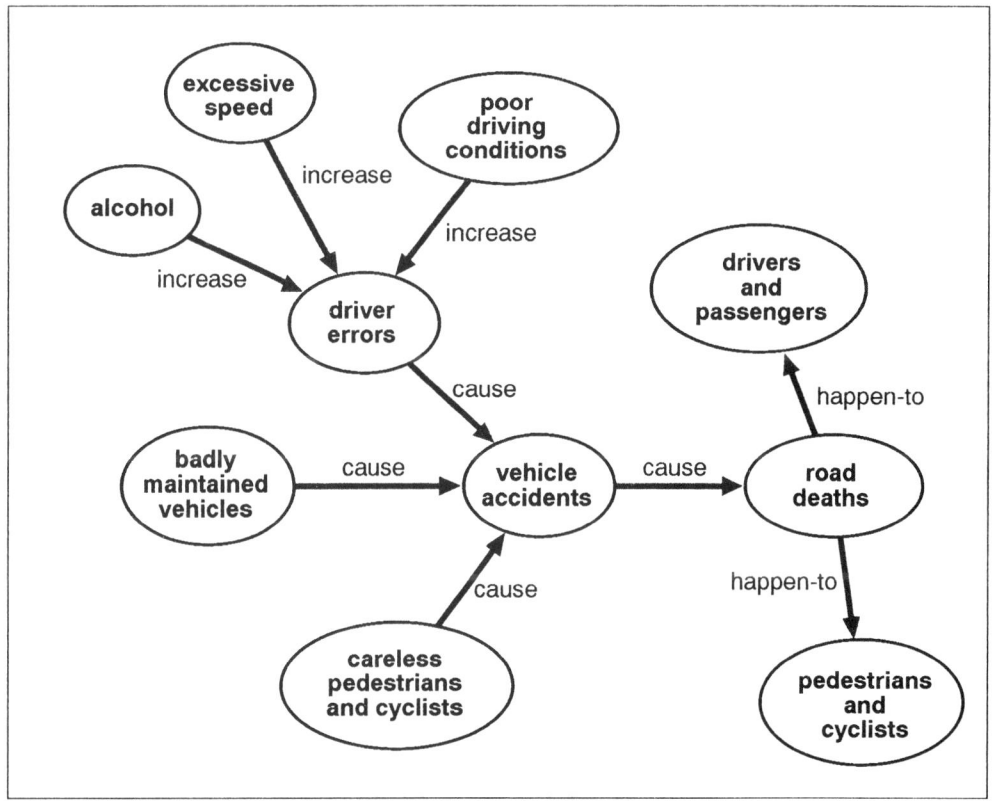

Figure 8.2 Semantic Net of one person's perspective on road accidents

Qualitative Models *Qualitative Models* define variables in terms of subjective judgements, for example high, normal or low, rather than prescribed numerical values. The qualitative model can be expressed in a form that is easily navigated by the Expert, through the use of a graphical interface. The technique is well suited to modelling complex systems, in particular for fault-detection applications.

For example, the structure of a piece of equipment can be modelled and, for each of its components, a range of acceptable states defined. A series of simulations can be run with a full range of component failures. Data is collected from these simulations and, using Rule Induction, a set of fault detection rules generated. It is, however, difficult to represent accurately the cumulative effect of several faults. Qualitative Modelling is only just becoming widely accepted although it is a potentially powerful technique.

8.4 KBS validation techniques

It is a common fallacy that validation can only take place once a system has been developed. For KBS, even more so than for conventional systems, there is a continual need to evaluate the represented knowledge against Expert opinion. This, in part, reflects the subjective nature of much of the expertise being modelled.

Because KBS present some particularly challenging validation problems, this section concentrates on KBS specific techniques. KBS projects also make use of the full range of conventional testing techniques, for example inspection, unit testing, integration testing and regression testing. To avoid confusion, each term is defined when it is first introduced.

Validation is defined as the process of determining whether a projected or current KBS product meets its requirements.

The guidance that follows is under the headings of Verification Techniques (objective validation) and Evaluation Techniques (subjective validation).

Chapter 8
Techniques

8.4.1 Verification Techniques

Verification is possible when a formal definition of the product requirement exists, for example, a specification against which the product can be objectively measured. Tools and approaches to support this process in KBS projects are by their nature heuristic, that is, based on rules-of-thumb rather than exhaustive. The existence of a specification does not imply that it is possible to build an exhaustive verification process.

The availability of appropriate test data is crucial to the implementation of verification activities. Test samples may have to be generated to ensure that there is sufficient coverage.

Static consistency checking

Static consistency checking involves ensuring that the representation of the knowledge base is internally consistent. Inspection is used to check that there are no conflicting definitions and that the product conforms to previous project documents from which it is derived.

A number of research tools exist for performing static checking of Knowledge Bases, but these are not yet generally available. It is expected that they will become available over the next few years. All tools pre-suppose that knowledge is captured in software, prior to checking. This is encouraging the adoption of more automated knowledge acquisition techniques.

Dynamic consistency checking

Dynamic consistency checking involves ensuring that no inconsistencies occur as a result of inferencing. This is a much bigger problem than dynamically testing conventional design or programs, due to the large number of states that a KBS can adopt. Care in design and coding can be used to cut down the number of paths through the envisaged system. Appropriate modularisation can help to reduce complexity, and simplify the testing and modification of code. Simple tracing of execution is often employed to test any parts of the design that are executable software.

GEMINI Technical Reference

Completeness
checking

Completeness checking involves confirming that all parts of the requirement have been addressed throughout the project. Unlike for most conventional systems, some ambiguity may continue to exist in specifications. However, the early checking of the mental processes that have been incorporated into the knowledge in Expertise Models provides an assurance that the system incorporates the correct functionality. Methods are beginning to appear that support completeness checking, for example the KOD method (see Annex B).

8.4.2 Evaluation Techniques

Evaluation is product validation against subjective criteria, for example, the performance of the Expert. Evaluation is used on a greater proportion of the products in a KBS project than on products in a conventional software development.

Knowledge Structure
Evaluation

If the *knowledge representation* is easy to understand, then this enables the Expert to evaluate the appropriateness of the knowledge structures. Mis-representation of the expertise is likely to be spotted earlier if the knowledge structures are accessible to the Expert. This is a highly subjective area, requiring as many experts as possible, together with a mechanism for reconciling any inconsistencies in their views. Depending on the form of representation used, it may be possible to display the structure of the knowledge graphically as an aid to evaluation.

Assessment of the
operational quality

The same process of identifying weaknesses and carrying out refinements is adopted with KBS as for conventional systems. Because of the cyclic nature of the development of a KBS, it is likely that significant refinements will be considered and evaluated throughout the development process.

Care is needed in managing the broad range of possible expert opinion on the quality of the system, for operational use. Specific acceptance criteria will have been defined. Whether the KBS is satisfactory largely depends on subjective assessments by experts and users of its effectiveness. Prior to implementation, assessments can be made of whether the planned or designed functionality will meet agreed performance criteria.

KBS are often judged in terms of competence. This is much more difficult to define and assess than whether a conventional system is functionally complete. However, it is this competence measure that is likely to determine whether a system is accepted by its users and provides the perceived benefits. For this reason, it is important that any tacit assumptions the User or Expert may have on the required competence level of the system are made explicit at an early stage.

8.5 Generally applicable techniques

The previous sections (8.2 to 8.4) looked at KBS specific techniques. KBS projects frequently make use of a variety of techniques employed in conventional systems development, some of which are discussed in section 8.5.1. Some general business analysis techniques, which are especially important in the early stages of projects, are discussed in section 8.5.2.

8.5.1 IT techniques

This section introduces a number of conventional IT techniques frequently used on KBS projects.

Prototyping

Prototyping is an umbrella term taking different forms depending on the overall objective. The following types of prototype have been identified within SSADM:

- demonstration prototyping
- requirements prototyping
- research prototyping
- specification prototyping.

Human Computer Interaction techniques

Many KBS projects have allowed user interface requirements to be over-constrained by the restrictions of KBS tools. Backward chaining systems are easier to implement using a system driven style of interaction rather than with the user in full control. However, this may conflict with organisational standards and prove unacceptable to users.

In order to overcome this, close attention has to be paid to the user-interface requirements. The full range of Human Computer Interaction techniques should be considered to ensure the system gains full approval of its users. These techniques include:

- *State Transition Models* to ensure that the interface provides the user with appropriate information and options for each state of the system

- *Workplace Models* to define how the envisaged system will integrate with the users' work-flow and the operational environment

- *Dialogue Design* to provide descriptions of the interface allowing the User to trace exactly how the system will be used

- *Style Guides* to document a common look and feel for all an organisation's systems.

Structured Walkthroughs

As KBS raise complex requirement and design issues at every stage, it is important that the entire project team is aware of these issues and has an opportunity to influence them. Depending on the level of technical awareness of the User and their availability, it is often desirable for them to be involved in *Structured Walkthroughs*. Decisions can be made immediately, based on their knowledge and discussions rather than via a lengthy referral process.

8.5.2 Other techniques

This section briefly describes a number of techniques that may be used on KBS projects but which are more general than the IT techniques described in section 8.5.1.

Soft Systems Methodology
: The *Soft Systems Methodology (SSM)* has been successfully applied to understand systems requirements, to improve business process and to manage change. In KBS projects, SSM is particularly useful for identifying requirements which cross organisational boundaries or for which there is no clearly identified consensus.

Cost benefit analysis
: *Cost benefit analysis* is an objective way of judging the merits of one option against another. Emphasis is on ensuring that all contributory factors are taken into account. With care, it can be extended to cover the quantification of non-financial benefits. These can be important in assessing business feasibility.

Impact analysis
: *Impact analysis* is used to describe the effect of pursuing a proposed technical, organisational or business course of action on the functional business environment. The technique can be applied to assess the impact of proposed KBS systems on the organisation, for example in terms of required changes to current procedures.

Decision analysis
: *Decision analysis* is a technique that involves taking an analytical approach to identifying the best action from a selection of possibilities, where the outcome of each is not known with certainty. The utility of each outcome as well as its probability is taken into account. Decision analysis can be used to determine whether it is more cost-effective to terminate or continue a project.

	Planning techniques	Conventional *planning techniques*, such as PERT and Gantt, can be applied to KBS projects. Effective resource estimation of the development activities depends upon the experience and skill of the planner.
	Risk modelling	During a KBS project there is a need to be aware of the internal project risks and the risks to the organisation of specific decisions. Conventional risk analysis techniques can be employed to do this.
8.6	Technique selection	Previous sections have described the range of techniques that may be appropriate to KBS projects. This section discusses the issues to be considered in the selection of techniques by reference to the main GEMINI development models. The contribution of techniques to the development of Management Products has been omitted as this is covered by standard management approaches.
8.6.1	General comments	GEMINI provides a framework for managing and controlling KBS development projects. It does not attempt to define all the ways in which information can be analysed and used within the project.

The project manager may decide to use a given technique for a variety of reasons, including:

- familiarity with the technique and recognising its fit with the planned development
- availability of tool support for the chosen technique, possibly reducing the cost of the project
- the nature of the requirements dictating the use of one specific technique
- the organisation's standardisation on particular techniques
- availability of specific skills.

Chapter 8
Techniques

All options should be considered fully and the basis of the decision recorded. Once techniques have been chosen for developing products, the activities to develop those products can be defined.

Significance of knowledge representation decision

The choice of *knowledge representation technique* is often one of the most significant decisions in the project as it can constrain the physical implementation. It can also influence the form of the knowledge acquisition techniques. A good choice of representation technique will enable the rapid definition of all necessary knowledge and its transformation into effective software. A bad choice may require a wasteful translation process or make unrealistic performance demands upon hardware. Several systems exist that exploit the strengths of more than one knowledge representation formalism to good effect.

Performance

Performance of the implemented system must be taken into account when selecting or using a particular technique. Often, the most appropriate knowledge representation is the one that will not make prohibitive demands on computer resources.

Review points

Some KBS specific techniques can be used for different activities in KBS development, from analysis and design through to implementation. It is important that there is a review of the relevance of the techniques for each activity and not blind adoption of the same knowledge representation techniques throughout.

Summary table	Figure 8.3 shows how the techniques, identified in section 8.2 to 8.5, may be employed in the development of the main GEMINI models.

The Logical Analysis Model is split into the two models that have gone into its construction. Section 8.6.7 discusses how these models can be merged. |
| Structure of section | Some of the key issues to be considered in the selection of appropriate techniques are discussed in the following text. To focus on the key areas, coverage is restricted to the following GEMINI development models:

- Business Domain Model
- Application Requirements Model
- Selected Application Model
- Modality Model
- Expertise Model
- Logical Analysis Model
- Functional Design Model
- Physical Design Model. |
| 8.6.2 Business Domain Model | The Business Domain Model requires:

- the development of a description of the business area for which a knowledge based system development is being considered
- identification of possible applications and an outline of each.

Production of the Business Domain Model is likely to be similar for KBS and non-KBS applications. An appreciation of the strategic business goals, organisational structures, current and envisaged workflow and the business processes these support is required by the project team. An understanding of the IT infrastructure and any over-riding IS-strategy is also required. |

Chapter 8
Techniques

Techniques \ Models	Business Domain	Selected Application	Application Requirements	Logical Analysis - Expertise	Logical Analysis - Modality	Functional Design	Physical Design
Knowledge Acquisition							
Exploratory Interviews	●	●	●	●	◐		
Structured Interviews	●	●	●	●	●	○	○
Case Analysis	◐	●	●	●	◐	○	○
Simulated Work		◐	○	●	●	○	○
Training		●	◐	●	○		
Questionnaires	○	◐	◐	●	◐		
Card Sorts		○	○	◐			
Repertory Grids		○	○	◐			
Wizard-of-Oz		○	○	◐	◐		
Telephone Test		◐	◐	◐	◐		
Manuals, Handbooks	◐	●	●	●	○		
Organisational Information	●	●	●	●	◐		
Textbooks	○	○	○	◐			
Rule Induction		◐	◐	◐		◐	◐
Statistical Analyses		◐	◐	◐			
Knowledge Representation							
Production Rules		○	○	●		●	●
Frames		○	○	●		●	●
First Order Predicate Logic		○	○	●		●	●
Contexts/Worlds		○	○	◐		◐	◐
Semantic Nets		◐	◐	◐		◐	◐
Certainty		○	○	◐		◐	◐
Qualitative Models		○	○	○		○	○
KBS Validation							
Static Consistency Checking			○	●	○	●	●
Dynamic Consistency Checking			○	●	○	●	●
Completeness Verification		●	●	●	●	●	●
Knowledge Structure Evaluation		○	○	●	○	●	●
Performance Assessment		○	○	●	○	●	●
General IT Techniques							
Prototyping		◐	◐	●	◐	◐	○
Task Analysis	○	◐	◐	●	●	◐	◐
Observation	●	●	●	●	●	◐	◐
Structured English/Pseudo Code		◐	◐	●	●	●	●
Simulation		○	○	◐	◐	●	●
Dataflow Models	○	◐	◐	●	●	●	●
Logical Data Models	○	◐	◐	●	●	●	●
State Transition Models		○	○	○	●	◐	●
Workplace Models	○	●	●	◐	●	◐	◐
Dialogue Design		◐	●	○	○	◐	●
Style Guides		○	◐	○	○	◐	●
Structured Walkthroughs		○	○	◐	●	●	●
Other Techniques							
Soft Systems Methodology	●	◐	●	○			
Cost Benefit Analysis	●	●	◐	◐			
Impact Analysis	●	●	●	○		○	○
Decision Analysis	●	◐	◐	○			
Planning Techniques	◐	◐	◐	◐	◐	◐	●
Risk Models	●	◐	◐	○	○		

● Extensive   ◐ Moderate   ○ Limited

Figure 8.3: Extent to which techniques typically contribute to main GEMINI Development Models

It is important that this model does not focus on the specifics of tasks, before business objectives and organisational requirements are defined. Criteria have to be established for the selection of specific applications. These criteria require strong management approval. Soft Systems Methodology (SSM) or other process improvement techniques are likely to be particularly important in ensuring general acceptance by management.

Exploratory and Structured Interviewing are the primary techniques used in building the model. The resulting overview of the business and possible applications have to be written in a form that is accessible to senior management. The source of different ideas and the identified levels of commitment have to be made explicit. A high-level appreciation of the dynamics of the organisation and its politics is essential, to ensure that the model captures real needs and that it can be communicated in the right way to the right audience.

Some consideration of technical feasibility normally takes place, which requires the use of staff experienced in the delivery of similar systems if it is to be effective. Summary descriptions of alternative applications and functionality are typically provided.

Extensive use of cost-benefit analysis and impact analysis is appropriate.

8.6.3 Application Requirements Model

The *Application Requirements Model* specifies the required external behaviour of the system together with the organisational, operational, technical and resource constraints on its implementation.

It is analogous to the top-level Requirements Specification of a conventional system. Exploratory and Structured Interviewing will be the most frequently used techniques to gain the necessary information.

Differing views in the Business Domain Model will have been consolidated into a coherent requirement. The organisational benefits associated with different functional options are clarified and documented in the Application Requirements Model. This enables management to make decisions on the options to be implemented.

Some use may be made of prototyping, typically to communicate to management the overall form of the proposed system.

A compact textual description of the requirement is frequently produced, with emphasis on covering the full range of organisational and business issues rather than functional and architectural detail.

Some task-level analysis, data flow modelling and logical data modelling may take place to help clarify key feasibility and scoping issues.

8.6.4 Selected Application Model

The *Selected Application Model* is the first real attempt to define the functionality of the proposed KBS in any detail. In particular, the expert and non-expert components are identified.

The model is used to extend the Development Team's understanding of the favoured business area down to the task level. Exploratory and Structured Interviewing are likely to be the primary techniques for gaining this information. Any of the knowledge acquisition techniques described in section 8.2 may be used to some extent.

Consideration of technical feasibility and risk involves examination of alternative knowledge representation techniques. Limited prototyping may take place to address areas of concern.

Data modelling and process modelling are likely to be undertaken. Detail of the organisational requirements must be determined, to ensure that all the envisaged interactions of the system have been considered. Conventional task and data flow modelling techniques are generally suitable.

Cost-benefit and impact analysis are used to define further the benefits case for the different functional options.

The emphasis in all the above techniques is on the production of a concise, well-formed definition of what is required:

- the benefits case
- feasibility
- costings
- risks.

This definition is normally documented in the form of a textual report with appendices providing high-level task models and risk assessment information.

8.6.5 Modality Model

The *Modality Model* represents the user view of the system and how it integrates with current or potential systems and with workflow. Some aspects of the interaction of system components may be transparent to the user.

Task modelling is the technique most frequently used to describe the envisaged activities. The resulting models can then be reviewed to identify which tasks are best built using KBS techniques, conventional techniques or manual methods.

Complex logical dependencies between parts of the system may be discovered at this stage, impacting earlier risk, cost and feasibility assessments. Performance requirements may require refinement if bottlenecks in workflow become identified as risks to overall objectives.

8.6.6 Expertise Model

The *Expertise Model* is the definitive model of the way that the problems or tasks within the scope of the KBS are currently solved. It is based upon extensive knowledge elicitation sessions with the Expert and draws together information which the Expert believes is appropriate for the application.

To produce it, the full range of knowledge acquisition and knowledge representation techniques should be considered. A variety of techniques, even competing ones, should be explored to ensure that the domain is viewed in the most appropriate way.

Expertise Models can be looked at from four perspectives:

- *domain data* which describes application terminology, together with facts, concepts and relationships pertaining to the application

- *inference knowledge* which describes the expertise that consists of the inference steps that are possible on the domain data, but without specifying their order or possible repetitions

- *tactical knowledge* which describes the structure of tasks required to solve an application problem. At the lowest level, it describes the sequences in which the inference steps can be performed to complete the task

- *strategic knowledge* which expresses the circumstances under which different task structures may be applied during problem solving.

The four perspectives may be captured using different techniques, as long as their compatibility is taken into account. Techniques suitable for domain data representation include entity-relationship diagrams and semantic nets.

Provisional decisions as to which Knowledge Representations, for example, Rules, Frames, or First Order Predicate Logic, are most appropriate influence the choice of knowledge acquisition techniques. Such decisions often influence subsequent decisions on which knowledge representations to use in the Functional Design Model. For these reasons the choice must be:

- made explicit and rejected options recorded

- reviewed critically during the production of subsequent models.

Some of the knowledge acquisition and representation techniques may result in runnable specifications or other machine-supported representations of the expertise. These can be made available to the Expert and User for validation and review.

KBS validation techniques are employed on the Expertise Model to ensure that it is internally consistent and consistent with the other models, also that it conforms to the Experts' knowledge.

8.6.7 Logical Analysis Model

The *Logical Analysis Model* is a synthesis of the Expertise Model and the Modality Model. Cross validation of these two models takes place.

Inconsistencies may arise when the Modality Model and the Expertise Model are brought together in the Logical Analysis Model. These inconsistencies can be minimised by constructing the two models in parallel and cross-checking them during construction. Inconsistencies may occur between the way tasks are carried out (decomposed) from the expert knowledge-oriented view and the user requirements-oriented view. The following inconsistencies may arise:

- tasks with different names

- different decompositions of the same task. There is often more detail in the Expert's decomposition

- tasks identified by Users having no equivalent tasks in Expertise Model derived from the Expert

- user tasks implicit in the Expertise Model not recognised in the Modality Model, for example, the provision of extra data about symptoms in a medical system

- different but overlapping definitions of tasks

- disagreement between User and Expert on how a task is carried out.

The resolution of these inconsistencies will involve inspection of the documents describing the two models. Direct discussion and negotiation involving the Expert and User may be necessary. The resulting Logical Analysis Model is built of a single set of tasks, which are understood by potential users and can be carried out using the knowledge elicited from the Expert.

Techniques which are directly applicable to the Logical Analysis Model include:

- structured English

- extended data flow modelling

- logical data modelling

- task modelling.

Structured walkthroughs of the model will take place. KBS validation techniques will be used to ensure that the model addresses its requirements.

8.6.8 Functional Design Model

The *Functional Design Model* is used to identify the main functional blocks of the final system. The resulting model and the way it is developed may well depend on the overall approach that is to be used in the implementation of the system, for example, rules or frames.

While the Functional Design Model is implementation independent, some thought must be given to implementation considerations to ensure that the Functional Design can be implemented efficiently and effectively.

The capabilities of different types of implementation tools and languages are considered. Their applicability for building the final system is assessed. Knowledge representation choices for the Functional Design Model can then be made, taking account of the usefulness for implementation of the chosen types of tool or language.

The external behaviour of a KBS reflects and is constrained by the choice of knowledge representation technique. The user interface may not need to map directly to the internal behaviour of the KBS and, therefore, be defined separately from the internal KBS and built using different tools. However, the user interface needs to be compatible with the internal KBS. Some representations can be used to define the required functionality by using structures which represent directly the way users and experts consider a problem. Some representations require the analyst to translate the expert and user views into a more formal specification. Choices on representations will have been made when building the Logical Analysis Model. However, a range of high-level functional design issues remains.

Performance assessment and risk assessment techniques will be applied to the range of available technical environment options. Conventional estimating techniques are also likely to be used.

Human Computer Interaction techniques can be used to define the user interface in some detail.

The Functional Design Model is verified against the Logical Analysis Model. Structured walkthroughs are likely to be used.

8.6.9 Physical Design Model

The *Physical Design Model* includes all the information required for coding to proceed.

The Physical Design Model is built by taking the Functional Design Model and Technical Environment Description and building a coherent, consistent, implementable model. The main purpose of the Physical Design activity is to ensure that the most effective design is built.

The issues to be taken into account during Physical Design include:

- specific characteristics of the selected tools and languages which may need to be reflected in the design

- the possible role of prototyping which may be used to address areas of technical uncertainty, for example, performance implications or physical integration problems. It may also be used to provide screen layouts in accordance with style guides

- performance modelling and capacity planning, though further detailed analysis may be completed during Physical Design.

Parts of the model are often defined using structured English and pseudo code. Use of State Transitions Diagrams are appropriate.

KBS Verification techniques and structured walkthroughs are also likely to be used.

8.7 Summary

A range of KBS-specific and more general techniques are likely to be used in KBS projects. The range of KBS techniques considered in this chapter has been restricted to those that are widely used with less frequently used techniques being identified in Annex B.

Following a brief description of techniques, this chapter has provided guidance on their selection. The chapter includes some general comments on techniques and their applicability in developing the main GEMINI development models. A key message of this chapter is the need to:

- consider the full range of available techniques
- make the basis of selection explicit
- review critically the decisions on which techniques to use as the project progresses.

Annexes

A Risk management issues

A.1 Categories of risk

It is necessary for all risks to a project to be identified and addressed if the project is to be successfully completed. In this way, managers can be assured that risks are under control and do not threaten the viability of the project and the quality of the results.

This annex provides a checklist for the different areas of risk which should be considered for any project.

The adoption of the spiral model highlights the need for continual risk assessment throughout a project. Issues of risk will vary depending upon the phase of the project has reached. The phases are:

- project initiation (section A.2)
- main development (section A.3)
- project closure and beyond (section A.4).

A further area for consideration is control of the demand/supply relationship (section A.5). This aspect may be relevant during any phase of the project and is documented separately.

Individual issues of risk are not restricted to a single phase of a project. The following checklist introduces the topics where they are likely to warrant most attention.

In each phase the topics of previous phases should be revisited and following phases checked to ensure that consideration is given to all relevant topics.

A.2	**Project initiation**	The Project Initiation Document contains details of risks to the project as they are perceived at that time.
	Tailoring GEMINI	The approach embodied in GEMINI should be tailored to meet the specific requirements of individual projects.

When tailoring GEMINI, Project Controllers should address the following in connection with risk management:

- definition of control points. Consideration should be given to the complexity of control procedures as well as the frequency of control activities
- adoption of the principles for project management embodied within the spiral model
- definition of development activities. Care is required to ensure that there are not too many levels or too many parallel activities to manage effectively
- specification of interaction between spirals
- definition of project goals.

General business impact

The business perspective of risk covers any issue which could be harmful to the business of the organisation. Issues concerning business risk may have implications wider than any single project. Risk should be managed to ensure that the project delivers the expected business benefits and does not adversely affect the business in any way.

Topics to address concerning impact on the business include:

- identification of the consequences of the project not succeeding

- identification of the external factors which affect the scope of the project and its likelihood for success. The external factors may include changes to legislation or to the business's financial situation

- assessment of inter-project dependencies and responsibility for controlling these dependencies. For example:

    - whether this project depends on other projects being completed successfully

    - whether other projects depend on this project being completed successfully

- assessment of how implementation of this system affects other functions necessary to support the business

- identification of implications of training staff to use, operate and maintain the KBS

- assessment of the overall approach that will be taken to maintenance of the KBS after implementation

- assessment of security protection requirements.

Project management   Topics to address concerning project management
                           include:

                           - setting realistic project objectives which are
                             attainable with the identified resources

                           - outlining high-level plans which are
                             realistic and of sufficient detail

                           - specifying the overall project organisation,
                             in terms of roles, including a clear
                             definition of:

                               - reporting lines

                               - delegated authority levels

                               - communication lines.

Project size and   Topics to address concerning the size and complexity of
complexity   the project include:

                           - estimation, in outline, of timescales and
                             effort. In particular, the size of the project
                             team and elapsed timescale

                           - distribution of the project team. Working
                             across several sites may cause
                             communications problems. Use of external
                             suppliers requires careful consideration
                             and management control

                           - identification of requirements for interfaces
                             to existing systems

                           - definition of the major development tasks
                             as a set of manageable activities.

Annex A
Risk management issues

Staffing
: Topics to address concerning staffing include:

  - identification of individuals to undertake the roles necessary to undertake the project
  - identification of skill requirements
  - consideration of training requirements and the need to recruit or buy-in external resources
  - arrangements for replacement staff should assigned personnel become unavailable.

Commitment
: Topics to address concerning commitment to the project include:

  - consideration of the commitment of the project sponsor, where one exists. The sponsor's view may dictate some of the objectives and requirements for the project
  - assessment of commitment from the management of the groups which are likely to be involved in the project
  - assessment of commitment of key individuals who are to be involved in the project.

Quality assurance
: Topics to address concerning quality assurance are:

  - identification of policy for version control
  - identification of policy for change control
  - identification of product assurance aspects, including the approach to be used for defining criteria for determining completeness
  - specification of an approach to testing and acceptance of the system
  - assessment of how users identify their criteria for the acceptability of the implemented system.

GEMINI Technical Reference

Application definition

Topics to address concerning application definition include:

- clear definition of the project terms of reference
- clear definition of the requirement
- definition of the benefits of the proposed system
- assessment of the scope of the project including:
  - defining the boundaries of the knowledge to be analysed
  - expertise availability and cost
  - coverage of both user requirements and expertise
  - identification of the embodied commonsense knowledge
- accessibility of the existing expertise
- volatility of the expertise
- availability of documentation of interfaces with other systems
- identification of standards for documentation (product development)
- identification of techniques to undertake the activities on the project.

A.3 Main development phase

The concerns for risk identified at project initiation provide information concerning areas for consideration during the rest of the project. The potential for deviating from previous risk resolution strategies must be assessed to ensure that the project is always correctly focused for the current situation.

Within the main development phase, there will be particular concerns for risk within each sector of the spiral model. The topics listed in section A.2 should be considered during this phase.

Annex A
Risk management issues

A.3.1 Risk assessment sector

Topics to address during the risk assessment sector include:

- critical assessment of the objectives set in the Project Initiation Document or the current Circuit Initiation Document
- awareness of implications of identified risks outside the current spiral and in spirals higher and lower in the spiral hierarchy
- control of changes
- any issues raised in the review sector.

A.3.2 Planning sector

Topics to address during the planning sector include:

- the impact that the results of the review of the risk assessment sector have on the activities which need to be scheduled
- derivation of estimates. Estimates should be done bottom-up based on a detailed understanding of the requirements, not top-down to fit into a predetermined timescale
- definition of the plans at the correct level for the purpose of the plan and the activities embodied
- clear definition of the products to be developed
- specification of suitable review criteria
- definition of the development tasks ensuring that there are not too many parallel activities

- compilation of a test plan and test data. This includes assessing if:
  - there are definable right answers in the domain or the problems being solved by the system have several acceptable answers
  - the Domain Team is able to provide a suitable range of test cases.

A.3.3 Development sector

General topics to address during the development sector include:

- assessing adherence to project objectives
- assessing adherence to agreed standards and procedures as documented in the quality plan
- availability of resources as scheduled during the planning sector
- identification of exception situations which may cause the project to fail
- deployment of an appropriate approach for:
  - knowledge acquisition
  - knowledge representation
  - building the system and, where appropriate, prototyping. In this context, issues include the use of tried and tested technology and assessment of vendor credibility.

Annex A
Risk management issues

KBS development	Topics to address concerning development of KBS include: • specification of, and adherence to, technical objectives • use of innovative techniques • specification of performance objectives • testing needs, including tests for reliability and usability as well as functionality.
System complexity	Topics to address concerning the complexity of the system being developed include: • complexity of the requirements • complexity of the application information and its quality • assessment of the implications of the stated technical objectives • assessment of the likelihood that the solution will require a mix of KBS and non-KBS technology.
System security	Security requirements of the implemented system may have to be considered if they are likely to affect the design decisions taken during development. Topics to address concerning security, particularly the IT components of the system, include: • assessing how to ensure the availability of data and expertise • assessing how to ensure the confidentiality of data and expertise • assessing how to ensure the integrity of the data and expertise • auditability of changes made to the data and expertise. CRAMM can be used to address these topics.

A.3.4 Review sector

Topics to address during the review sector include:

- preparation for review activities
- availability of reviewers
- suitability of review criteria
- communication with other spirals
- definition of clear objectives for further work.

A.4   Project closure and beyond

There must be an assessment of the project on completion. The KBS will be installed and used to support the business.

Topics to address during the final phase of the project and the subsequent lifetime of the system include:

- definition and control of the processes for handover
- definition and control of the processes for implementation
- assessment of the impact the implemented system will have on other operational systems
- specification of system maintenance requirements to enable this function to be carried out effectively and efficiently
- assessment of which aspects of this project were well-done to provide information for future projects.

Annex A
Risk management issues

A.5 Demand-supply relationship

Some activities for a project may be undertaken by individuals external to the demand side. In this situation, there are several topics to address. The formality to which these are documented depends on the relationship between the demand and supply sides. Topics to address concerning the relationship between the demand and supply sides include:

- identification of the potential supply side. For example:
  - whether the supplier is internal to the business organisation
  - whether there are complications concerned with the use of external suppliers
- assessment of the supply side approach to quality and the need for this approach to accord with the demand side approach
- assessment of the proposal
- adequacy of provisions for review and acceptance
- assessment of implications of the relationship. For example:
  - legal implications such as ownership of intellectual property rights
  - implementation and maintenance implications
- clear divisions of responsibility
- communication mechanisms
- working relationships
- escalation procedures.

B Techniques list

This annex provides:

- *definitions* of a number of KBS techniques that are not considered widely enough used to be included in Chapter 8
- *references* to further information on the above techniques as well as those considered in Chapter 8. Full references to publications can be found in the bibliography of this manual, under *Techniques references*.

Techniques for which the reader should refer to the main body of the text are shown in bold type.

Analogical Reasoning	Reasoning by analogy refers to reasoning across different domains in order to exploit structural similarities between them.
Assumption-Based Truth Maintenance System (ATMS)	*ATMS* is a technique that attempts to maintain beliefs in lines of reasoning. Technically, the assumptions are propositions whose belief depends on the disbelief of other propositions. See De Kleer (1986).
Belief Logic	*Belief Logic* seeks to represent the basis of agents' decisions. See Hobbs and Moore (eds) (1985).
Card Sorts	See Kidd (ed) (1987), Hart (1986) and Diaper (1989).
Case Analysis	See Kidd (ed) (1987), Hart (1986) and Diaper (1989).

Case Based Reasoning	*Case Based Reasoning* involves gathering together data relating to the way agents or organisations behave over time with respect to a given decision-making process or business process. When a new occurrence of a problem takes place, similar past cases are extracted and presented to the KBS user. The user may need to consult an expert to apply these cases to the current problem. A variety of similarity measures exist, giving a variety of ways of combining cases to design new solutions.
Certainty	See Jackson 1990.
Completeness Checking	See Hollnagel (1989) and Balci, O'Keefe and Smith (1987).
Contexts/Worlds	*Context and Worlds* are used in representations that exhibit hypothetical reasoning. Rich (1983) provides a detailed description of the search techniques that can be employed. See also ATMS and JTMS entries.
Dempster-Schafer Evidence Theory	Dempster-Schafer techniques are a way of handling uncertainty that involves distributing belief measures across a number of hypotheses. Unlike Bayesian techniques, belief measures do not have to be allocated to each member of the set of hypotheses. See Nilsson (1986).
Documentary Sources	See Kidd (ed) (1987), Hart (1986) and Diaper (1989).
Dynamic Consistency Check	See Hollnagel (1989) and Balci, O'Keefe and Smith (1987).

Epistemic/Autoepistemic Reasoning	Epistemology is concerned with the theory of knowledge. *Epistemic reasoning* focuses on the structure, derivation and reliability of knowledge. Thus, an epistemic system is able to make statements about the way it derives its conclusions. Autoepistemic knowledge contains information on its own structure, derivation and production.
Exploratory Interviews	See Kidd (ed) (1987), Hart (1986) and Diaper (1989).
First Order Predicate Logic (FOPL)	See Brachman and Levesque (1985), Jackson (1990) and Ringland and Duce (1988).
Frames	See Brachman and Levesque (eds) (1985), Jackson (1990) and Ringland and Duce (eds) (1988).
Fuzzy Logic	*Fuzzy Logic* is a technique for handling uncertainty. Graphs are defined showing the spread of possible values for variables that do not have discrete values. The graphs also define the categorisation of the possible values into particular sets. The storage and manipulation of fuzzy sets can be prohibitive in terms of the amount of computation required. Simplifying assumptions often have to be made to implement fuzzy logic systems. See Mamdani and Gaines (1981).
Human Computer Interaction techniques	See Helander (1988), Schneiderman (1986) and Brown (1988).
Justification-Based Truth Maintenance Systems (JTMS)	*JTMS* is a form of representation often used in hypothetical reasoning which involves a non-monotonic reasoning strategy, that is one in which statements are not required to hold true throughout the reasoning process. A JTMS involves recording each proposition, the other propositions from which it is derived and also those propositions that have been excluded. See Doyle (1979).

KADS Method	The *KADS Method* was derived from an EC funded research project involving the University of Amsterdam and a number of commercial organisations. It is in use by a number of consultancy organisations. See Hickman (1988).
Knowledge Structure Evaluation	See Hollnagel (1989) and Balci, O'Keefe and Smith (1987).
KOD Method	The *KOD Method* is a commercially available method with its own prescribed software lifecycle model. The method incorporates a number of KBS validation tools.
Modal Logics	*Modal Logics* are those systems of logic that are based on ideas of necessity and possibility. See Charniak and McDermott (1985) and Chellas (1980).
Multi-Agent Modelling	*Multi-Agent Modelling* is an Artificial Intelligence Technique that seeks to model groups of decision-makers, their organisational structures, the protocols they employ to communicate, their knowledge and beliefs and the way in which they co-operate to arrive at decisions. A feature of multi-agent modelling is that it adopts a consistent approach, regardless of whether the operations are carried out by humans or by intelligent systems. See Huhns (1987).
Non-Monotonic Reasoning	*Non-Monotonic Reasoning* refers to a reasoning process or logical system, where information that is true in a given context may be made untrue by something that happens to that context, requiring the retraction of a whole line of reasoning. In monotonic reasoning, by contrast, something that is asserted as true remains true. See Rich (1983).

Annex B
Techniques list

Object Orientation	The object-oriented paradigm is an approach to modelling which builds on ideas of abstract (real world) objects, encapsulation and class inheritance.

- An *object* contains both data, represented by attributes, and processing, represented by methods. The 'object' behaves (performs a task) in response to receiving a message that it understands

- A *method* is an internally coded procedure which implements (part of) the functionality of an object. It is actioned when the object receives a specific message

- *Encapsulation*, also known as 'information hiding', ensures that the internal structure of an object is invisible to all other objects. Encapsulation isolates the object data and methods from the outside world. All communication between objects is in the form of messages

- A *message* is the mechanism by which one object communicates with another to force the execution of a method

- A *class* is used to define common attributes and methods for a group of objects. The "class object" can be considered as a parent of the (child) objects it relates to. A child may have more than one parent

- *Inheritance* is the hierarchic mechanism by which "child" objects exhibit behaviour and properties defined by their forebears.

See Booch (1991), Meyer (1988) and Rumbaugh (1991).

Production Rules	See Jackson (1990) and Ringland and Duce (1988).

Prototyping	See Ledgard and Taver (1987), Wilson and Rosenberg (1988) and Connell and Brice Schafer (1989).

Qualitative Models	See Brachman and Levesque (1985).

Repertory Grids	See Kidd (1987), Hart (1986) and Brachman and Levesque.
Rule Induction	See Hart (1986).
Semantic Nets and Conceptual Graphs	See Ringland and Duce (1988).
Simulated Work	See Kidd (ed) (1987), Hart (1986) and Diaper (1989).
Situation Calculus	*Situation Calculus* is a form of logic system that enables statements to be defined as true within certain states or snapshots. Events are regarded as transitions between states and explicit rules can be defined to indicate the content of the transitions. See McCarthy and Hayes (1969).
Soft Systems Methodology	See Checkland and Scholes (1990) and Wilson (1990).
Spatial Reasoning	*Spatial Reasoning* is the term used for a group of techniques addressing problems such as:

- the translation of graphical to textual information
- the processing of inputs from visual sensors to form 3-dimensional representations.

Approaches to spatial reasoning include Spatial Logics (see Fleck 1987) and Shape Grammars (Stiny 1980). Demand in the area of Geographical Information Systems is providing impetus to the development of such techniques.

Static Consistency Checking	See Hollnagel (1989) and Balci, O'Keefe and Smith (1987).

Annex B
Techniques list

Structured Interviews   See Kidd (ed) (1987), Hart (1986) and Diaper (1989).

Task Analysis   See Diaper, D (1987) and Phillips, Bashinki, Ammerman and Fligg (1988).

Temporal Logics   *Temporal Logics*, typically an extension of First Order Predicate Logic, are used for representing statements such as "B was true at some time in the past" or " C will be true at some time in the future". Reasoning over time remains an extremely difficult area of knowledge representation. See Allen (1982).

Validation   See Hollnagel (1989) and Balci, O'Keefe and Smith (1987).

Bibliography

CCTA Publications

PRINCE	*PRINCE Reference Manuals*, NCC Blackwell Ltd, (1990), ISBN: 1 85554 012 6
SSADM	*SSADM Version 4 Reference Manuals*, NCC Blackwell Ltd (1990), ISBN: 1 85554 004 5
CRAMM	An *Overview of CRAMM* (1992) is available from the CCTA Library.
Information Systems	The Information Systems Guides, published by John Wiley & Sons Ltd, Baffins Lane, Chichester PO19 1UD.

The following set of guides is referenced in this publication:

- *CCTA IS Guides Set B: Systems Development Set*, ISBN: 0 471 92556 X

Information Systems Engineering Library

The Information Systems Engineering Library provides guidance on managing and carrying out Information Systems Engineering activities. Relevant publications published by HMSO:

- *Improving the Maintainability of Software* (1993) ISBN: 0 11 330585 0

The foundation volumes of the GEMINI guidance consist of three volumes:

- *GEMINI: Controlling KBS Development Projects - Guidance for business-side project controllers*, ISBN: 0 11 330591 5

- *GEMINI: Managing KBS Development Projects - Guidance for IS-provider project managers*, ISBN: 0 11 330592 3

- *GEMINI Technical Reference - Guidance for KBS development project teams*, ISBN: 0 11 330593 1

Quality Management Library	The Quality Management Library (1992), published by HMSO as a five volume boxed set, ISBN: 0 11 330569 9
Appraisal and Evaluation Library	The Appraisal and Evaluation Library is a set of volumes which helps organisations to identify the products, particularly software, which best meet their requirements. Relevant volumes are: • *Overview and Procedures (1990)*, ISBN 0 11 330534 6 • *Knowledge Based Systems (1990)*, ISBN 0 11 330570 2
IT Infrastructure Library (ITIL)	ITIL is a series of books about how to provide quality IT services, and on the accommodation and environmental facilities needed to support IT. Relevant titles include: • *Capacity Management (1991)*, ISBN: 0 11 330544 3 • *Configuration Management (1989)*, ISBN: 0 11 330530 3 • *Change Management (1990)*, ISBN: 0 11 330525 7 • *Testing an IT Service for Operational Use (1993)*, ISBN: 0 11 330560 5

Bibliography

Other Publications

Boehm, BW, *A Spiral Model of Software Development and Enhancement*, Computer, May 1988

Ernst & Young US, *Ernst & Young Navigator System Series^{SM} Methodology Overview Monograph*, Ernst & Young, (1990)

Ernst & Young, *STAGES - Structured techniques for the analysis and generation of expert systems*, Ernst & Young (1991)

Hickman et al, *Analysis for knowledge-based systems: a practical guide to the KADS methodology*, Ellis Horwood, (1989)
ISBN: 0 7458 0689 9

PA Consulting Group, *How to take part in the quality revolution: a management guide*, PA Consulting Group. (Undated)

Taylor et al, *CONCH: a spiral life-cycle model for KBS development, Report G, Esprit Project 1098*, Touche Ross (1989)

Wilson, Systems: *Concepts, Methodologies and Applications*, Wiley (1990),
ISBN: 0 471 92716 3

Allied Quality Assurance Publication	AQAP, AQAP - 13: *Nato Software Quality Control System Requirements.* (1981)
International Organization for Standardization	ISO, *ISO 9001 - Quality Systems: Specification for design/development, production, installation and servicing (also known as British Standard BS5750, Part 1*, British Standards Institution, (1987).

Techniques references

Allen, J (1982): *Maintaining knowledge about temporal intervals*. Communications of the ACM, 26, 832-43.

Balci, O, O'Keefe, R M, Smith, E (1987): *Validating Expert System Performance*. IEEE Expert, Winter 1987, 81-89.

Booch, G (1991): *Object Orientated Design with Applications*, Benjamin Cummings,
ISBN: 0 8053 00910

Brachman, R J and Levesque, H J (eds) (1985): *Readings in Knowledge Representation*, Morgan Kaufmann, Los Altos,
ISBN: 0 934613 01 x

Brown, C M (1988): *Human-Computer Interface Design Guidelines*, Ablex, Norwood NJ.
ISBN: 0 89391 332 4

Charniak, E and McDermott, DV (1985): *Introduction to Artificial Intelligence*. Addison-Wesley
ISBN: 0 201 11946 3

Chatfield, C and Collins, A J (1980): *Introduction to Multivariate Analysis*, Chapman and Hall,
ISBN: 0 412 16040 4

Checkland, P and Scholes J (1990): *Soft Systems Methodology in Action*, J Wiley, Chichester,
ISBN: 0 471 92768 6

Chellas, B, (1980): *Modal Logic*, Cambridge University Press,
ISBN: 0 521 29515 7

Connell, J L and Brice Schafer, L (1989): *Structured Rapid Prototyping*,
ISBN: 0 13 853573 6

De Kleer, J (1986): *An Assumption-based Truth Maintenance System*. Artificial Intelligence, Vol 28, 1987, 127-162.

Diaper, D (1989): *Knowledge Elicitation*, Ellis Horwood, Chichester,
ISBN: 0 7458 0451 9

Doyle, J (1979): *A Truth Maintenance System*, Artificial Intelligence Vol 12, 231-272.

Fleck, M M (1987): *Representing Space for Practical Reasoning*, IJCAI 87.

Hart, A (1986): *Knowledge Acquisition for Expert Systems*, Kogan Page, London,
ISBN: 1 85091 091 X

Helander, M (ed) (1988): *Handbook of Computer Interaction*, Elsevier,
ISBN: 0 444 70536 8

Hobbs, J and Moore, R (eds) (1985): *Formal theories of the common sense world*. Norwood NJ: Ablex,
ISBN: 0 89391 213 1

Hollnagel, E (1989): *Evaluation of Expert Systems*. This is one paper within this book which is a collection of papers. Guida and Tasso (eds) (1989): Topics in Expert System Design, Amsterdam: North Holland Publishing Co.,
ISBN: 0 444 87321 X

Huhns, M N (ed) (1987): *Distributed Artificial Intelligence*. Morgan Kaufmann.

Jackson, P (1990): *Introduction to Expert Systems*, Addison-Wesley,
ISBN: 0 201 17578 9

Kidd, A L (ed) (1987): *Knowledge Acquisition for Expert Systems - a practical handbook*, Plenum Press, London,
ISBN: 0 306 42454 1

Ledgard, H and Taver, J (1988): *Professional Software, vol 1 Software Engineering Concepts*, Addison-Wesley,
ISBN: 0 201 12231 6

Mamdani, E H and Gaines, B R (1981): *Fuzzy Reasoning and its applications*, Academic Press,
ISBN: 0 12 467750 9

McCarthy, J and Hayes, P in Meltzer, B and Michie, D (eds): *Machine Intelligence 4*, Edinburgh University Press.

Meyer, B (1988): *Object-Orientated Software Construction*, Prentice-Hall,
ISBN: 0 13 629031 0

Nilsson, N J (1986): *Probabilistic Logic Artificial Intelligence Vol 28 No 1 Feb 1986*.

Phillips, M, Bashinki, H, Ammerman, H and Fligg, C (1988): *A Task Analytic to Dialogue Design*, in Helander (ed) (1988)

Rambaugh, J, Blaha M, Premer, L W, Frederick, E, Lorenson, W: *Object-Orientated Modelling and Design*, Prentice-Hall,
ISBN: 0 13 630054 5

Rich, E (1983): *Artificial Intelligence*. McGraw Hill,
ISBN: 0 07 052261 8

Ringland, G A and Duce, D A (eds) (1988): *Approaches to Knowledge Representation - an introduction*, Wiley,
ISBN: 0 905451 78 3

Shneiderman, B (1986): *Designing the User Interface: Strategies for Effective*,
ISBN: 0 20 57286 9

Stiny, G (1980): *Introduction to Shape and Shape Grammars. Environment and Planning B, Vol 7*.

Wilson, B (1990): *Systems, Concepts, Methodologies and Applications*, J Wiley, Chichester,
ISBN: 0 471 92716 3

Wilson, J and Rosenberg, D (1988): *Rapid Prototyping for User Interface Design*, in Helander (ed) (1988)

Glossary

activity	The process of creation, or further development, of a product. Each time a product is to be created or enhanced, an activity is defined to effect the transformation.
activity description	Documentation of an activity. It is a description of the activity which includes its purpose and the required inputs, outputs and skills required to undertake the activity.
agent	A person or other system that interacts with or is a component of the KBS.
Application Requirements Model	The product that holds a specification of the required external behaviour of the system, together with the organisational, operational, technical and resource constraints which affect the way that the system is to be designed and implemented.
BAC	See Business Assurance Co-ordinator.
Business Assurance Co-ordinator (BAC)	A role within the Project Assurance Team that is responsible for planning, monitoring and reporting on all administrative aspects of the project. The role acts as the focal point for administrative controls.
Business Domain Model	The product that provides an understanding of the organisational structure and business functions. This understanding allows the scope of possible applications to be identified. The impact of a possible system on the organisation can be clarified and defined. For potential applications the Business Domain Model covers both current and proposed systems and requirements.
CCTA Risk Analysis and Management Method (CRAMM)	A method which provides a structured and consistent basis to identify and justify all the protective measures necessary to ensure the security of both current and future IT systems used for processing data.

Checkpoint Report	A report prepared by the Project Manager, with help from the PAT, to summarise project progress which is passed to the Project Controller.
Circuit Initiation Document (CID)	The product which gathers together the information needed to control the work which is to be undertaken during a circuit of the spiral model. This information includes defining the objectives and boundaries of the activities.
Configuration Librarian	The role responsible for planning, monitoring and reporting on all configuration management aspects of the project.
configuration management	A set of techniques and procedures to record, monitor and control the status of pre-defined items which must be developed through the lifetime of the project.
CRAMM	See CCTA Risk Analysis and Management Method.
deliverables	Products which must be developed by the supply side and formally accepted by the demand side. These products must be defined in terms of content, structure and format.
demand side	The business areas within an organisation which make demands upon the IS provider(s) for the provision of information systems and services.
Development Team	The team responsible for developing the products of specific development activities within a project.
Domain Team	The team responsible for providing information for use in analysis and design activities. The team is made up of the User and Expert roles.
estimating	Calculating the approximate size of a task in terms of required resources, cost and timescale.
Executive	A role within the Project Board (usually the chairman) responsible for ensuring that the project objectives are met and that the project is completed within the approved cost and timescales.

Glossary

Exception Plan	The product which documents the details of an exception situation which has arisen, or is likely to arise, including extremes that have been examined or considered, and proposes corrective action.
expert	A person who has detailed understanding in the domain of knowledge for which the KBS is to be designed. The role, *Expert*, is undertaken by a group of experts, or their representative, who provide information, during analysis and design, by interviews or by documentary evidence such as manuals or case studies.
Expertise Model	The product which holds a structured description of the knowledge (expertise) to be encoded into the implemented KBS.
Feasibility Report	The final report resulting from a feasibility study. The Feasibility Report forms the basis of management decisions about the future of the system under study.
Feasibility Study (FS)	This activity generates an initial assessment of the feasibility of building a system in the area of business which has been identified by a strategy study or project review activities.
Functional Design Model	The product which reflects design decisions concerning how individual components of the system will be implemented. It is a revision of the Logical Analysis Model.
Human-Computer Interaction (HCI)	All aspects of the interaction between computers and their users.
knowledge acquisition	A term commonly applied to the process by which KBS project teams gain an understanding of the knowledge in the business area of concern.
knowledge based systems (KBS)	Computer systems which are characterised by their ability to hold and make available knowledge in a specific domain.
Knowledge Engineer	The role of development personnel in a KBS project. They carry out the analysis, design and programming activities for a KBS development.

knowledge representation	The formalisms that are adopted to record expertise in a structured form.
Logical Analysis (LA)	This activity specifies precisely what is needed to meet the requirements without being constrained by how the requirements are to be met.
Logical Analysis Model	The pivotal product in a GEMINI-based project. It brings together the Expertise Model and the Modality Model into a single validated whole.
Logical Design (LD)	This activity completes and checks all aspects of the design before implementation issues are considered in Physical Design.
Management Risk Assessment	The product used to document the risk assessment undertaken during the risk assessment sector of the spiral model.
Modality Model	The product which defines interactions in the proposed system. *Agents* are persons or processes that interact with or are components of the proposed system. The Modality Model identifies the agents, defines which tasks each performs and how they can ask for or give information. The pattern of interaction between agents is termed *modality*.
object orientation	The object-oriented paradigm is an approach to modelling which builds on ideas of abstract (real world) objects, encapsulation and class inheritance.

- An *object* contains both data, represented by attributes, and processing, represented by methods. The 'object' behaves (performs a task) in response to receiving a message that it understands

- A *method* is an internally coded procedure which implements (part of) the functionality of an object. It is actioned when the object receives a specific message

- *Encapsulation*, also known as 'information hiding', ensures that the internal structure of an object is invisible to all other objects. Encapsulation isolates the object data and methods from the outside world. All communication between objects is in the form of messages
- A *message* is the mechanism by which one object communicates with another to force the execution of a method
- A *class* is used to define common attributes and methods for a group of objects. The "class object" can be considered as a parent of the (child) objects it relates to. A child may have more than one parent
- *Inheritance* is the hierarchic mechanism by which "child" objects exhibit behaviour and properties defined by their forebears.

See Booch (1991), Meyer (1988) and Rumbaugh (1991).

PAT	See Project Assurance Team.
PBS	See Product Breakdown Structure.
PFD	See Product Flow Diagram.
Physical Design (PD)	This activity generates the Physical Design Model in sufficient detail to enable development of the operational system.
Physical Design Model	The product which represents all the components and functions of the system to be implemented. It is implementation dependent, the design details being dependent on the technical environment chosen for implementation.
Physical Environment Specification	The product which specifies the hardware and software products and services to be supplied, commissioned and made available for implementation.
Physical System Specification	The product that draws together the Physical Design Model and the Physical Environment Specification.

PID	See Project Initiation Document.
PIR	See Post Implementation Review
plan	The product that documents the results of the planning process. It shows targets in terms of products, resources required, timescales and quality. It shows how the resources identified have been scheduled to meet these targets.
planning	The process of estimating, collating, sequencing and scheduling the project's resources to deliver the required products.
Post Implementation Review (PIR)	A formal mechanism to determine the extent to which a completed project has met its objectives and realised the expected benefits. It generally takes place about 6 months after implementation.
PRINCE	A government developed method for project management with particular application to the management of Information Systems projects. It is a development of the PROMPT method which has been in use in government departments since 1983.
product	Any output from a project. The output may be an item of software, hardware, or documentation and may itself consist of a number of detailed products. In GEMINI, products are described within three main categories: *Management Products* (which are produced during the management of a project), *Technical Products* (which are those products that make up the system) and *Quality Products* (which are produced for, or by, the quality process).
Product Breakdown Structure (PBS)	The product which identifies the products which are required and must be produced by a project. It describes the system in a hierarchic way, decomposing it through a number of levels down to the components of each product.
product description	The product which describes the purpose, form and components of a product, and lists the quality criteria which apply to it.

Glossary

Product Flow Diagram (PFD)	The product which is used to describe the technical strategy of a project in terms of a diagram showing the products of the project and how they are derived from each other. It is essentially a working document produced by planners for their own benefit.
production management	The activities to administer all the resources needed to develop the Technical Products which are required to fulfil the objectives of the project.
product quality review	A means whereby a product (or group of related products) is checked against an agreed set of quality criteria. Those criteria are defined for every product (on the product description) and may be supplemented with other documents.
Progress Report	The product which is used to report back to management details of the current status of the project, highlighting relevant issues.
Project Assurance Team (PAT)	The team that assists the Project Controller by ensuring that the project products are fit for their intended purpose and conform to specification. The PAT must ensure that quality management is undertaken within the project. The Project Assurance Team comprises: • Business Assurance Co-ordinator (BAC) • Technical Assurance Co-ordinator (TAC) • User Assurance Co-ordinator (UAC).
Project Board	A group of senior managers within the demand side organisation who have an interest in, and overall control of, the KBS project. The Project Board must provide overall guidance and direction to the project. The Project Board comprises: • Executive • Senior User • Senior Technical.

Project Controller	The demand side project manager responsible for the success of the project in terms of the quality of the delivered system, budget and timescale. The Project Controller acts on behalf of the Project Board, has close links with the board members and attends board meetings.
Project Evaluation Report	The product which provides an indication of how successful the project has been in all its various aspects.
project integration	The development of an implementable system which combines KBS and conventional IT. Integration may involve techniques for the analysis and design, or techniques and tools for implementation.
Project Initiation Document (PID)	The product approved by the Project Board at project initiation; it defines the terms of reference and objectives for the project. It is used to identify business requirements, as well as organisational and general information needs, security aspects and an initial Project Plan.
project management	The activities to administer all resources to develop products which are required to fulfil the objectives of the project.
project management process model	An iterative approach to project management for KBS development projects. This model incorporates four sectors concerning the activities of risk assessment, planning, development and review.
Project Manager	A role with day-to-day responsibility for ensuring that the supply side produces the required products, to the required standard of quality, within specified constraints of time and cost.
project organisation	The composition of a project team in terms of the skills and experience required to undertake all of the necessary functions of control, management and development within a project.
QA	See quality assurance.
QAS	See quality assurance statement.

Glossary

quality	Quality is defined in ISO 8402 as: *the totality of features and characteristics of a product or service that bear on its ability to satisfy stated or implied needs.*
quality assurance (QA)	The scope of quality assurance is described in ISO 8402 - 1986. It covers: *all those planned and systematic actions that provide adequate confidence that a product or service will satisfy given requirements for quality.*
quality assurance statement (QAS)	This product documents the quality approach for the project. It is developed by the Project Controller to specify quality issues which must be addressed throughout the project.
quality control	The mechanisms to encompass the operational techniques and activities for use in satisfying the project and product requirements.
quality criteria	The identifiable characteristics of a product that are to be examined to determine whether the product meets stated requirements and can be considered fit for its purpose. These characteristics are documented in a product description for each product.
quality management	The practice of a variety of tasks which for individual projects, assure and control development activities through the use of various techniques, including reviews, walkthroughs and inspections.
quality review	An examination to confirm that products conform to their specification. Errors found in products are documented and corrected.
Requirements Analysis (RA)	This activity specifies requirements early in the project to establish a sound basis for design and acceptance.

Review Team	A group of people who undertake the quality review of a product. There will be a chairman for the Review Team as well as a presenter (originator of the material to be reviewed). The remainder of the team includes people who must assess the product from a particular perspective to ensure that it is fit for purpose.
risk	In a project *risk* is the likelihood, and impact, of a project *failing* to: • meet a business need and provide expected business benefits • prove technically feasible • prove organisationally feasible • complete on time and within budget • develop products which meet requirements.
risk assessment	The process of identifying risks, evaluating their impact and identifying countermeasures.
risk management	The process by which risks, inherent in a project and its environment, are identified, understood, analysed and addressed.
role	One of the discrete project functions required to manage and carry out a project. Roles are assigned to individuals according to the needs of the project and the mix of skills available.
Selected Application Model	The product which provides a representation of the tasks and data flows in an application. This representation provides a more precise definition of the functionality of the proposed application than the Business Domain Model.
Senior Technical	The role on the Project Board that represents the interests of demand side areas which have responsibility for technical implementation of the KBS, and for computer services support during its operational life.

Glossary

Senior User	The role on the Project Board that represents the interests of all user departments and functions affected by the project. In addition, the Senior User monitors project progress against the business requirements of user management.
spiral model	See project management process model.
supply side	Those responsible for providing information systems to meet the needs of the demand side business.
system maintenance	All activities concerned with making any change, however small, to an existing computer system.
System Modelling (SM)	This activity defines the business environment around the proposed application in detail so that the application impact on the business can be established accurately.
TAC	See Technical Assurance Co-ordinator
Team Leader	The role responsible for managing a Development Team and specific resources during the development of particular products.
Technical Assurance Co-ordinator (TAC)	The role within the Project Assurance Team responsible for planning, monitoring and reporting on all technical assurance aspects of the project. The role ensures that the technical and operating standards defined for the project and its products are used to good effect.
Technical Environment Definition (TE)	This activity generates a detailed assessment of the technical environment for implementation of the application.
Technical Environment Description (TED)	This product contains a definition of the requirements of the environment in which the application is to be developed and will run.
Technical Environment Options	This product describes the reasonable options for the implementation of the system, in sufficient detail to support choice.
TED	See Technical Environment Description.

GEMINI Technical Reference

UAC	See User Assurance Co-ordinator.
user	Any person who uses a system for business purposes. The role, *User*, is undertaken by a group of users, or their representative, who provides information, during analysis and design, on user requirements and may be involved in testing.
User Assurance Co-ordinator (UAC)	The role within the Project Assurance Team responsible for monitoring and reporting on the user assurance aspects of the project. In addition, the role represents the user on a day-to-day basis.
work structure	A diagram that shows the activities, and flows of products, which must be undertaken to develop the required project products.

Index

activities	2.1, 2.4.3, 4.1, 6.1, 6.3, 7.1.1
activity	
description	5.1, 5.4, 6.1, 6.5, Chapter 7
details	5.4.2
agents list	5.13.2
analogical reasoning, see techniques	
analysis	
cost/benefit, see techniques	
decision, see decision analysis in techniques	
errors, see techniques	
impact, see techniques	
requirements, see Requirements Analysis	
task, see techniques	
application definition	A.2
Application Requirements Model	3.4.2, 4.8, 5.5, 8.6.3, Fig 8.3
Application Product, see products	
assumption-based truth maintenance system (ATMS), see techniques	
belief logic, see techniques	
Business Domain Model	3.4.2, 4.8, 5.6, 8.6.2, Fig 8.3
card sorts, see techniques	
case	
analysis, see techniques	
based reasoning, see techniques	
CCTA Risk Analysis and Management Method (CRAMM)	1.6
certainty	8.3, Annex B
Checkpoint Reports	4.5
Circuit Initiation Document	4.5, 5.7
commitment	A.2
completeness checking, see techniques	
composition and/or breakdown	5.2.3, 5.19.2
conceptual graphs, see techniques	
contexts/worlds, see techniques	
control points	6.1, 6.4
cost/benefit analysis, see techniques	
CRAMM, see CCTA Risk Analysis and Management Method	

data flow modelling, see techniques
decision analysis, see techniques
delivery environment   5.5.2
demand side   2.1, 3.2, A.5
demand/supply relationship   A.5
Dempster-Schafer, see techniques
development
    environment   5.5.2
    models   3.4.2, 4.2
    sector   3.3.2, A.3.3
    Sector Plan, see plans
    Team   3.2.3, 3.2.5
diagrams
    conventions   4.3
    notation   6.3.1
documentary sources, see techniques
domain   3.4.3
    data   5.8.2
    Team   3.2.3
dynamic consistency checking, see techniques

Education Products, see products
Education Guide   4.6
Education Strategy   4.6
epistemic/autoepistemic reasoning, see techniques
error analysis, see techniques
evaluation, see techniques
evidence theory, see techniques
Exception Plan, see plans
Expert   3.2.3, 8.2.1
Expertise Model   3.4.2, 4.8, 5.8, 8.6.6, Fig 8.3
exploratory interviews, see techniques

Feasibility   7.2
    Report   4.8, 5.9, 7.2
    Study   3.4.2, 7.2
financial assessment   5.9.2
First Order Predicate Logic (FOPL), see techniques
flexibility   2.2
FOPL, see techniques
Frames, see techniques
Functional Design Model   3.4.2, 4.8, 5.10, 7.6.5, 8.6.8, Fig 8.3

fuzzy logic, see techniques

Index

Handover Products, see products
HCI techniques, see techniques
Highlight Report   4.5
human-computer interaction (HCI), see techniques
human expert, see expert
Human Factors, see products

impact analysis, see techniques
inference knowledge   5.8.2
initial review   3.3.2
interaction model   5.13.2
interviews
    exploratory, see techniques
    structured, see techniques
IT Infrastructure Library (ITIL)   1.6

JTMS, see techniques
justification-based truth maintenance systems (JTMS), see techniques

KADS, see techniques
KBS validation, see techniques
knowledge
    acquisition, see techniques
    definition   3.4.3
    Engineer   3.2.5
    evaluation, see techniques
    inference, see inference knowledge
    representation   3.4.1, 8.3, 8.6.1
    strategic, see strategic knowledge
    structure evaluation, see techniques
    tactical, see tactical knowledge
    transformation   2.4.3, 3.4.1
KOD method, see techniques

Logical
    Analysis   7.5
    Analysis Model   3.4.2, 4.8, 5.11, 7.5.5, 8.6.7, Fig 8.3
    data modelling, see techniques
    Design   7.6

Maintenance Products, see products
Management Products, see products
modal logics, see techniques
Modality Model   3.4.2, 4.8, 5.13, 8.6.5, Fig 8.3
Multi-Agent Modelling, see techniques

non-monotonic reasoning, see techniques

object orientation, see techniques
operating environment   5.5.2
Operating Guide   4.6
Operations Products, see products

PFD, see Product Flow Diagram
Physical
    Design   7.8
    Design Model   4.8, 5.14, 7.8.5, 8.6.9, Fig 8.3
    Environment Specification   4.8, 5.15
    System Specification   4.8, 5.16
planning sector   3.3.2, A.3.2
plans   4.5, 5.17
    Development Sector Plan   4.5, 5.17.1
    Exception Plan   4.5, 5.12.2, 5.17.1
    Project Plan   4.5, 5.9.2, 7.2.5
    quality plan   4.7, 5.17.2
    resource plan   5.17.2
    technical plan   5.17.2
product
    Breakdown Structure   Chapter 4, 5.18
    description   4.1, 4.7, Chapter 5, 5.19, 6.3.3
    description format   5.2
    Flow Diagram   5.20, 6.1, 6.2
production rules, see techniques
productivity level   5.21.2
product-oriented framework   2.4.3, 3.1, 3.4
Products   Chapter 5, 6.3.1
    Application Products   4.6, 4.8
    Education Products   4.6
    Handover Products   4.6
    Human Factors   4.6
    Maintenance Products   4.6
    Management Products   2.4.3, 4.4, 4.5
    Management Risk Assessment   4.5, 5.12
    Operations Products   4.6
    Quality Products   2.4.3, 4.4, 4.7

	Security Risk Assessment	4.6
	Technical Products	2.4.3, 4.4, 4.6
	User Products	4.6
Progress Reports		4.5, 5.21
project		
	achievements	5.21.2
	Board	3.2.1, 4.5
	boundary	5.22.2
	closure	A.4
	Controller	3.2.2
	definition	5.22.2
	environment	5.5.2
	Evaluation Report	4.5
	Initiation Document	4.5, 5.22, A.2
	management	3.3, 5.21.2, A.2
	management process model	2.4.2, 3.1, 3.3
	manager	3.2.4
	organisation	2.4.1, 3.1, 3.2, 5.22.2
	plan, see plans	
	risk	2.1, 3.3.2
	scope	4.1
	size	A.2
prototyping, see techniques		
pseudo code, see techniques		
QAS, see quality assurance statement		
qualitative models, see techniques		
quality		2.2, 3.3.2, 5.2.5
	assurance statement (QAS)	4.7, 5.22.2, A.2
	criteria	5.2.5
	plan, see plans	
	review	4.7, 5.2.5
questionnaires, see techniques		
Rejected Technical Environment Options		4.8, 5.9.2, 5.23
Release Package		4.6
repertory grid, see techniques		
Requirements Analysis		7.3
resolution options		3.3.2, 5.12.2
resource plans, see plans		
review		
	participants	7.1.2
	sector	3.3.2, A.3.4
rigour		2.2

risk, see project risk
    assessment   4.5, 5.12
    assessment sector   3.3.2, A.3.1
    categories   A.1
    identification   5.12.2
    management   5.12, Annex A
    management issues   Annex A
    modelling   8.5.2
roles   3.1, 3.2
rule induction, see techniques

Selected Application Model   3.4.2, 4.8, 5.24, 8.6.4, Fig 8.3
semantic nets, see techniques
Service Level Agreement   4.6
simulated work, see techniques
simulation, see techniques
situation calculus, see techniques
soft systems method, see techniques
spatial reasoning, see techniques
spiral model, see project management process model
staffing   A.2
static consistency checking, see techniques
statistical analysis, see techniques
strategic knowledge   5.8.2, 8.6.6
structured
    english, see techniques
    interviews, see techniques
    walkthrough, see techniques
supply side   2.1, 3.2, A.5
system
    complexity   A.3.3
    security   A.3.3
    testing   4.7

tactical knowledge   5.8.2
task analysis, see techniques
task model   5.13.2
Team Leader   3.2.5
technical
    Environment Definition   7.7
    Environment Description   4.8, 5.25
    Environment Option   5.26
    exceptions   4.7
    Plan, see plans
    Products, see products

Index

techniques	6.3.3, Chapter 8
analogical reasoning	Annex B
assumption-based truth maintenance system (ATMS)	Annex B
belief logic	Annex B
card sorts	8.2.1, Annex B
case analysis	8.2.1, Annex B
case based reasoning	Annex B
completeness checking	8.4.1, Annex B
conceptual graphs	8.3, Annex B
contexts/worlds	8.3, Annex B
cost/benefit analysis	8.5.2
data flow modelling	5.8.2, 8.5.1
decision analysis	8.5.2
Dempster-Schafer	Annex B
derivation from data	8.2.3
documentary sources	8.2.2, Annex B
dynamic consistency checking	8.4.1, Annex B
epistemic/autoepistemic reasoning	Annex B
error analysis	5.21.2
evaluation	8.4.2
evidence theory (Dempster-Schafer)	Annex B
exploratory interviews	8.2.1, Annex B
First Order Predicate Logic (FOPL)	5.8.2, 8.3, Annex B
Frames	8.3, Annex B
fuzzy logic	Annex B
general	8.5
human-computer interaction (HCI)	8.5.1, Annex B
impact analysis	8.5.2
IT	8.5.1
justification-based truth maintenance systems (JTMS)	Annex B
KADS Method	Annex B
KBS validation	8.1, 8.4
knowledge acquisition	8.2
Knowledge structure evaluation	8.4.2, Annex B
KOD method	Annex B
logical data modelling	5.8.2, 8.5.1
modal logics	Annex B
Multi-Agent Modelling	Annex B
non-monotonic reasoning	Annex B
object orientation	Annex B
observation	8.5.1
other	8.5.2

techniques (cont.)
- participant observation — 8.5.1
- planning — 8.5.2
- production rules — 5.8.2, 8.3, Annex B
- prototyping — 8.5.1, Annex B
- pseudo code — 5.14.2, 8.5.1
- qualitative models — 8.3, Annex B
- questionaires — 8.2.1
- repertory grid — 8.2.1, Annex B
- rule induction — 8.2.3, Annex B
- selection — 8.6
- semantic nets — 5.8.2, 8.3, Annex B
- simulated work — 8.2.1, Annex B
- simulation — 8.5.1
- situation calculus — Annex B
- soft systems method — 8.5.2, Annex B
- spatial reasoning — Annex B
- special — 2.1
- static consistency checking — 8.4.1, Annex B
- statistical analysis — 8.2.3
- structured english — 5.8.2, 5.14.2, 8.5.1
- structured interviews — 8.2.1, Annex B
- structured walkthrough — 8.5.1
- task analysis — 8.5.1, Annex B
- telephone test — 8.2.1
- temporal logics — Annex B
- validation — 8.4, Annex B
- verification — 8.4.1
- wizard of oz — 8.2.1

telephone test, see techniques
temporal logics, see techniques
test plan — 7.6.5
training — 8.2.1

usability — 2.2, 3.2.3
User — 3.2.3
User Products, see products

validation, see techniques
verification, see techniques

wizard of oz, see techniques
work structure — 2.4.3, 5.27, Chapter 6
work structure notation — 6.1, 6.2